eXtreme Life

eXtreme Life
A Quiet Time Journal
For Preteens

An Imprint of
DISCIPLESHIP PUBLICATIONS INTERNATIONAL

EXTREME LIFE
Kingdom Kids Curriculum © 1998
Discipleship Publications International
One Merrill Street, Woburn, MA 01801

All Scripture quotations, unless indicated, are taken from the
HOLY BIBLE, NEW INTERNATIONAL VERSION. Copyright © 1973, 1978, 1984
by the International Bible Society. Used by permission of Zondervan Publishing House.
All rights reserved.

The "NIV" and "New International Version" trademarks are registered
in the United States Patent Trademark Office by the International Bible Society.
Use of either trademark requires the permission of the International Bible Society.

All rights reserved. No part of this book may be duplicated, copied, translated,
reproduced or stored mechanically or electronically without specific, written permission of
Discipleship Publications International. Sharing of the material in this book with other churches
or organizations not owned or controlled by the original purchaser is also prohibited.

Printed in the United States of America

Cover Design: Chad Crossland, Chris Costello
Interior Layout: Chris Costello, Anita Costello

Kingdom Kids and Generation Next are trademarks of DPI

ISBN 1-57782-079-7

CONTENTS

Before You Start 7

Quarter 1: Fall 1

Unit 1: Evidences
Week 1: Is There a God? 8
Week 2: How We Got the Bible 11
Week 3: Our Guide to Life 14
Week 4: Prophecies Fulfilled 17
Week 5: Jesus Is God 20

Unit 2: Guts and Glory
Week 6: Courage to Follow 23
Week 7: Dealing with Fear 26
Week 8: Conviction 29
Week 9: Against the Crowd 32
Week 10: Helping One Another 35

Unit 3: The Character of Jesus
Week 11: The Humility of Jesus 38
Week 12: The Conviction of Jesus 41
Week 13: The Joy of Jesus 44

Quarter 2: Winter 1

Unit 4: The Great Commission
Week 14: Compassion 47
Week 15: Entrust to Reliable Men 50
Week 16: Whatever the Cost 53

Unit 5: The Uniqueness of Jesus
Week 17: He Is God 56
Week 18: He Is Creator 59
Week 19: He Is Judge 62
Week 20: He Is Human 65

Unit 6: Proverbs
Week 21: Discipline 68
Week 22: Speech 71
Week 23: Living Wisely 74
Week 24: Things God Hates 77
Week 25: Materialism 80
Week 26: Humility 83

Quarter 3: Spring 1

Unit 7: Friendship
Week 27: Spiritual Relationships 86
Week 28: Peer Pressure 89
Week 29: Being a Team 92
Week 30: Building Deep Relationships 95
Week 31: Communication 98

Unit 8: Changed Lives
Week 32: Samaritan Woman 101
Week 33: Zacchaeus 104
Week 34: Lydia 107
Week 35: The Ethiopian 110

Unit 9: Family
Week 36: The Plan 113
Week 37: Marriage 116
Week 38: Respect 119
Week 39: Resolving Conflict 122

Quarter 4: Summer 1

Unit 10: The Character of Jesus II
Week 40: Compassion 125
Week 41: Self-control 128
Week 42: Patience and Forgiveness 131
Week 43: Anger 134
Week 44: Thankfulness 137

Unit 11: Evidences II
Week 45: Medical Science and the Bible 140
Week 46: Physical Science and the Bible 143
Week 47: Archaeology and the O.T. 146
Week 48: Archaeology and the N.T. 149

Unit 12: Crucifixion and Resurrection
Week 49: Fulfilled Prophecies 152
Week 50: The Garden and the Trial 155
Week 51: The Cross 158
Week 52: The Resurrection 161

Looking Back, Looking Ahead 164

BEFORE YOU START

We called this book *Extreme Life* because there is nothing lame about being a disciple of Jesus. It takes great courage, determination and strength. It is not easy at times, but it is always right and always rewarding. The life of a disciple is the best life of all: We have the best Father and the best friends in the world. We know who we are living for. We have great fun. And on top of it all, we get to go to heaven and be with God and his people forever!

This quiet time book goes along with your Sunday and midweek classes. It will help you to apply what you are learning to your normal, everyday life.

Make a decision to spend time with God in his word every day and to write a brief response to the question. Pray the prayer that is given to help you focus, but pray about other things as well: your family, your example at school, schoolwork, sharing Jesus with friends, struggles or questions, etc. Talk to God about whatever is on your heart.

Each week write down your Weekly Challenge in the appropriate space. Then write what you did to meet that challenge.

Nothing is more important in your day than these minutes spent with God each morning. But if for some reason you get behind on your studies, start fresh each week with the new lesson so you keep up with what is being taught in your class at church.

When you have been using the book for a week or so, show your parent(s) or another older Christian what you have been doing. See if they have any suggestion to help you get more out of your time with God.

Have a great time with God each day, and learn more about the Extreme Life he calls us to live (and helps us to live). Never forget, God is your greatest fan.

Write your name here so your book will not end up in another preteen's hands:

IS THERE A GOD?

MEMORY VERSE: Isaiah 40:26

> Lift your eyes and look to the heavens:
>   Who created all these?
> He who brings out the starry host one by one,
>   and calls them each by name.
> Because of his great power and mighty strength,
>   not one of them is missing.

DAY 1 REVELATION 4:9-11

QUESTION: Why is the Lord worthy to receive glory, honor and power?

_____
_____
_____

PRAYER FOR THE DAY: God, help me honor you with my life today.

Did you know? There are more stars in the universe than grains of sand on earth.

DAY 2 ISAIAH 45:11-12

QUESTION: Name three things that God has created.

_____
_____
_____

PRAYER FOR THE DAY: God, thank you for making all the stars in the sky!

Did you know? Our galaxy, the Milky Way, contains 100 billion stars—so large of a number that counting one star every second would take 2,500 years!

WEEK 1

**U1 L1
Evidences**

DAY 3 DEUTERONOMY 32:5-6

QUESTION: Why were these people foolish and unwise?

_____
_____
_____

PRAYER FOR THE DAY: God, help me *never* turn from your ways, for you are my Father in heaven and my Creator.

Did you know? The closest star to our solar system, other than our sun, is about 25 trillion miles away? If you could go the speed of light, which is 186,000 miles per second, it would take you 1.5 seconds to reach the moon, about 8 minutes to reach the sun and a little over 4 years to reach this star (Proxima Centauri)!

DAY 4 PSALM 139:13-14

QUESTION: How well does God know you? Why?

_____
_____
_____

PRAYER FOR DAY: God, thank you for creating me and knowing me even before I was born!

Did you know? The largest stars known are called "supergiants." Some have the *diameter* of the distance from our sun to Saturn!

DAY 5 EPHESIANS 2:10

QUESTION: Can you name three good works that you have been created to do?

_____
_____
_____

PRAYER FOR THE DAY: God, help me to do good works today.

Did you know? The brightest stars are one million times brighter than our sun!

IS THERE A GOD?

**U1 L1
Evidences**

DAY 6 ISAIAH 40:28-31

QUESTION: What are some things God can do for you?
_____
_____
_____

PRAYER FOR THE DAY: God, you are my Creator. Help me turn to you and trust you always.

Did you know? The interior temperature of an average star is millions of degrees Fahrenheit!

DAY 7 ROMANS 1:18-20

QUESTION: Why is it just an excuse when people say they do not believe in God?
_____
_____
_____

PRAYER FOR THE DAY: God, help me to share with others why I believe you exist.

Did you know? A shooting star is a meteor's rapid fall to the earth.

WEEKLY CHALLENGE

(WRITE YOUR WEEKLY CHALLENGE AND HOW YOU FULFILLED IT.)

IS THERE A GOD?

U1 L1 Evidences

HOW WE GOT THE BIBLE

MEMORY VERSE: Psalm 119:89

Your word, O Lord is eternal;
it stands firm in the heavens.

DAY 1 PSALM 119:159-160

QUESTION: Why isn't there anything in the Bible that is false?

_____
_____
_____

PRAYER FOR THE DAY: God, help me to love your word.

Did you know? It took about 1,600 years to complete the Bible. The earliest book was written about 1,500 years before the birth of Jesus, and the last book was written 75 years after.

DAY 2 PSALM 119:152

QUESTION: God's plan is for the Bible to last forever. Do you believe that the Bible can help you today as much as it helped people many years ago? Why?

_____
_____
_____

PRAYER FOR THE DAY: God, please help me to learn something from your word every day in my quiet times.

Did you know? Before printing presses and photocopiers were invented, books and letters were copied by hand! Scribes had to carefully count every letter of every page and book to compare it to the original. Imagine having to copy the entire Bible by hand! How long do you think that would take?

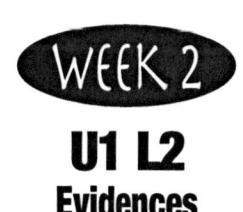

WEEK 2

U1 L2
Evidences

DAY 3 ISAIAH 40:8

QUESTION: How long does this scripture say that God's word will last? How does this encourage you?

_____
_____
_____

PRAYER FOR THE DAY: Lord, please help me to remember and to be thankful that your word will last forever.

Did you know? Ancient manuscripts of the Old Testament were written not on paper, but on prepared animal skins or leather!

DAY 4 MATTHEW 5:18

QUESTION: Jesus said that everything in God's law will be accomplished. How does that make you feel?

_____
_____
_____

PRAYER FOR THE DAY: God, please help me to always tell the truth to everyone, just as Jesus did.

Did you know? The Bible was originally written in Aramaic, Hebrew and Greek.

DAY 5 PSALM 12:6

QUESTION: Look up the word "flaw" in the dictionary. What does it mean? What does the word "flawless" mean?

_____
_____
_____

PRAYER FOR THE DAY: God, please help me to remember that the Bible is flawless; it is perfect!

Did you know? There are more copies of the New Testament (more than 40,000) in existence today than any other ancient writing.

HOW WE GOT THE BIBLE

WEEK 2

U1 L2
Evidences

DAY 6 2 PETER 1:16

QUESTION: How do you feel when someone tells you something exciting that they have seen with their own eyes? Why do you tend to believe an eyewitness?

_____
_____
_____

PRAYER FOR THE DAY: God, please help me to realize that what I read in the Bible is not make-believe but the Truth!

Did you know? There are enough quotations from the early church leaders that, even if we didn't have a single copy of the New Testament, scholars could reconstruct all but eleven of its verses!

DAY 7 1 PETER 1:23-25

QUESTION: There is a quote from the Old Testament in the passage. Can you give the book and chapter?

_____
_____
_____

PRAYER FOR THE DAY: God, please help me to let your word live through me.

Did you know? Voltaire, a famous writer of the 1700s, predicted that the Bible would be gone in 100 years. But 50 years after he died, his printing press was used to print Bibles, and his home was turned into a center for distributing them.

WEEKLY CHALLENGE
(WRITE YOUR WEEKLY CHALLENGE AND HOW YOU FULFILLED IT.)

HOW WE GOT THE BIBLE

U1 L2 Evidences

OUR GUIDE TO LIFE

MEMORY VERSE: 1 Timothy 4:16

Watch your life and doctrine closely. Persevere in them, because if you do, you will save both yourself and your hearers.

DAY 1 JUDGES 21:25

QUESTION: What do you think life in Israel was like with everyone doing as they pleased? What would it be like in your family?

_____
_____
_____

PRAYER FOR THE DAY: God, help me to live by your word today, and not by my feelings.

Did you know? The Bible is the world's longest standing best-seller.

DAY 2 PROVERBS 14:12

QUESTION: What does this proverb say about the "way that seems right to a man"? What would the result be in living this way?

_____
_____
_____

PRAYER FOR THE DAY: God, help me to do what is right in your eyes and not my own.

Did you know? The Bible was the first ever book to be printed mechanically.

U1 L3
Evidences

DAY 3 ISAIAH 45:19

QUESTION: According to this verse, who declares what is right? How does this make you feel?

_____
_____
_____

PRAYER FOR THE DAY: God, I am so grateful that you have given us a book of truth—the Bible!

Did you know? A Gutenberg Bible set the world record for the most valuable book. It was sold at an auction in 1978 for almost 2 million dollars!

DAY 4 HOSEA 14:9

QUESTION: Are you walking in the ways of the Lord or stumbling in them? Are you righteous or rebellious?

_____
_____
_____

PRAYER FOR THE DAY: God, help me be a righteous person who walks and does not stumble in your ways.

Did you know? The Bible is the world's most widely distributed book, with nearly 3 billion copies published since 1819!

DAY 5 JOHN 8:31-32

QUESTION: What will be the result of knowing the truth? What does it mean to be set free?

_____
_____
_____

PRAYER FOR THE DAY: God, help me to hold to your teaching today and therefore, to know the truth!

Did you know? Complete books of the Bible have been published in 1,763 different languages and dialects—worldwide!

OUR GUIDE TO LIFE

WEEK 3

DAY 6 PSALM 119:120

QUESTION: What does it mean to be in awe of God's laws?
_____
_____
_____

PRAYER FOR THE DAY: God, help me be in awe of your word today.

Did you know? The Bible covers a span of 2,000 years of human history.

DAY 7 HEBREWS 4:12-13

QUESTION: Why is the word of God like a sword? How is the Bible "living" in your daily life?
_____
_____
_____

PRAYER FOR THE DAY: God, help me to use the Bible as my guide when I have problems or questions.

Did you know? The Bible has changed millions of lives and revolutionized entire countries.

WEEKLY CHALLENGE
(WRITE YOUR WEEKLY CHALLENGE AND HOW YOU FULFILLED IT.)

OUR GUIDE TO LIFE

WEEK 3

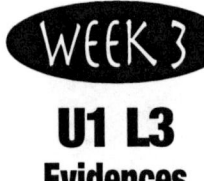

U1 L3
Evidences

PROPHECIES FULFILLED

MEMORY VERSE: Isaiah 46:10

"I make known the end from the beginning,
   from ancient times, what is still to come.
I say: My purpose will stand,
   and I will do all that I please."

DAY 1 MATTHEW 7:17-18

QUESTION: What kind of fruit does your life produce? Are you a living example of Jesus?

_____
_____
_____

PRAYER FOR THE DAY: God, help me to bear good fruit and be a good example to my friends and family.

Did you know? The phenomenon of fulfilled prophecy is one of the main proofs that the Bible is the very word of God. No other religious documents, such as the Muslim Koran or the Book of Mormon, have such a way to prove themselves.

DAY 2 ISAIAH 6:8

QUESTION: Is your attitude toward God the same as the prophet Isaiah? ("Here am I. Send me!")

_____
_____
_____

PRAYER FOR THE DAY: God, give me the desire to always do what you want.

Did you know? Isaiah's name means "The Lord is salvation." Isaiah was one of Israel's greatest prophets whom God used to call the people to change their lives.

WEEK 4

**U1 L4
Evidences**

DAY 3 JEREMIAH 1:-8

QUESTION: What was Jeremiah called to be? Why was he afraid?
_____
_____
_____

PRAYER FOR THE DAY: God, thank you that you can use me, even though I am young.

Did you know? Jeremiah's name means "The Lord throws." Jeremiah is known as "The Weeping Prophet" because he was not afraid to express what he felt.

DAY 4 DANIEL 6:10

QUESTION: Why did Daniel keep praying to God?
_____
_____
_____

PRAYER FOR THE DAY: God, please help me to have the same faith as Daniel.

Did you know? Daniel's name means "God is my Judge." God gave Daniel the wisdom to interpret dreams.

DAY 5 JONAH 1:15-17

QUESTION: Jonah was running away from God. Why do you think Jonah would not do what God wanted him to do? What kinds of things do you think he thought about while he was in the fish?
_____
_____
_____

PRAYER FOR THE DAY: God, please help me to never run away from you!

Did you know? Pagans often offered human sacrifices to try to control the powers of nature.

PROPHECIES FULFILLED

WEEK 4

**U1 L4
Evidences**

DAY 6 JOSHUA 1:6-9

QUESTION: Why do you think God told Joshua so many times to be strong and courageous?

_____
_____
_____

PRAYER FOR THE DAY: God, thank you that you give me what I need to overcome all of my fears.

Did you know? Joshua's name means "The Lord saves." Joshua was a military commander under Moses.

DAY 7 GENESIS 6:11-14, 22

QUESTION: What do you think would have happened if Noah had not obeyed God?

_____
_____
_____

PRAYER FOR THE DAY: God, thank you for all of the examples you give us of obeying, and teach me how to obey willingly, like Noah.

Did you know? When God flooded the earth, only eight people survived.

WEEKLY CHALLENGE
(WRITE YOUR WEEKLY CHALLENGE AND HOW YOU FULFILLED IT.)

PROPHECIES FULFILLED

**U1 L4
Evidences**

JESUS IS GOD

MEMORY VERSE: **Colossians 2:9**

For in Christ all the fullness of the Deity lives in bodily form.

DAY 1 COLOSSIANS 1:15-17

QUESTION: What role did Jesus play in the creation?

_____
_____
_____

PRAYER FOR THE DAY: God, please help me to remember Jesus in everything I do and to have confidence that he is with me wherever I go.

Did you know? Jesus never wrote a book, had a family, owned a home, went to college, or traveled more than 200 miles from where he was born. Yet no one person has affected our lives more than he did!

DAY 2 JOHN 17:20-23

QUESTION: How did Jesus describe his relationship with God?

_____
_____
_____

PRAYER FOR THE DAY: God, please help me to be as unified with my friends in the church as Jesus was with God.

Did you know? During the time of Jesus' life, boys began preparing to become part of the religious community at age 12. Jesus amazed the religious teachers at the temple in Jerusalem when he himself was this age!

WEEK 5

U1 L5
Evidences

DAY 3 HEBREWS 1:1-4

QUESTION: Who is an "exact representation" of God?
_____
_____
_____

PRAYER FOR THE DAY: God, please help me to know Jesus so I can know you.

Did you know? Jesus is the only recognized religious leader who has ever claimed to be God...and the only one who performed miracles and rose from the dead to prove it!

DAY 4 JOHN 10:31-33

QUESTION: Why did the Jews want to stone Jesus?
_____
_____
_____

PRAYER FOR THE DAY: God, help me to be like Jesus and never be afraid to speak the truth.

Did you know? Jesus was not an only child; he had at least seven siblings! Can you imagine ten people sharing a small house?

DAY 5 JOHN 14:9-11

QUESTION: What is Jesus teaching Philip?
_____
_____
_____

PRAYER FOR THE DAY: God, help me to remember the miracles of Jesus so that I can believe that you and he are one.

Did you know? Our yearly calendars are based on Jesus' birth. B.C. means "Before Christ" and A.D. means "Anno Domini" which in Latin means "in the year of our Lord."

JESUS IS GOD

**U1 L5
Evidences**

DAY 6 JOHN 12:44-46

QUESTION: When you look at Jesus, who else do you see?

_____
_____
_____

PRAYER FOR THE DAY: God, help me to follow Jesus today as my light.

Did you know? Half of the population of the Roman Empire at the time of Christ were slaves. Yet the spread of Christianity eventually ended slavery!

DAY 7 MARK 6:1-6

QUESTION: Why do you think people in Jesus' hometown got angry at him because of his teaching?

_____
_____
_____

PRAYER FOR THE DAY: God, help me to honor you with my life today.

Did you know? More poems have been written, more stories told, more pictures painted and more songs sung about Christ than any other person in history!

WEEKLY CHALLENGE
(WRITE YOUR WEEKLY CHALLENGE AND HOW YOU FULFILLED IT.)

JESUS IS GOD

**U1 L5
Evidences**

COURAGE TO FOLLOW

MEMORY VERSE: I Kings 18:21

Elijah went before the people and said, "How long will you waver between two opinions? If the Lord is God, follow him; but if Baal is God, follow him."

DAY 1 I KINGS 18:36-39

QUESTION: How did Elijah display courage?
___
___
___
___

PRAYER FOR THE DAY: Lord, help me to imitate Elijah's heart throughout this week.

DAY 2 PSALM 27:1

QUESTION: Why should you be fearless?
___
___
___
___

PRAYER FOR THE DAY: Lord, teach me to be fearless and to trust in you today.

WEEK 6

**U2 L1
Guts and Glory**

DAY 3 ACTS 4:29

QUESTION: To whom do you need to speak boldly today?

_____
_____
_____
_____

PRAYER FOR THE DAY: Lord, help me to speak boldly about what is right to my friends today.

DAY 4 DEUTERONOMY 31:6

QUESTION: Why should you always count on God?

_____
_____
_____
_____

PRAYER FOR THE DAY: Lord, thank you for always being with me.

DAY 5 2 THESSALONIANS 3:13

QUESTION: How do you feel when you do what is right?

_____
_____
_____
_____

PRAYER FOR THE DAY: Lord, help me to please you in every way today.

COURAGE TO FOLLOW

WEEK 6

**U2 L1
Guts and Glory**

DAY 6 ACTS 20:24

QUESTION: Have you completed the challenge given to you in class this week? Why do you think it is good to have specific challenges?

_____
_____
_____
_____

PRAYER FOR THE DAY: Lord, thank you for giving me courage this week.

DAY 7 LUKE 23:34

QUESTION: Is there someone you need to forgive?

_____
_____
_____
_____

PRAYER FOR THE DAY: Lord, I forgive those who did not understand my love for you this week.

WEEKLY CHALLENGE
(WRITE YOUR WEEKLY CHALLENGE AND HOW YOU FULFILLED IT.)

COURAGE TO FOLLOW

U2 L1
Guts and Glory

DEALING WITH FEAR

MEMORY VERSE: Philippians 4:13

I can do everything through him who gives me strength.

DAY 1 I KINGS 19:9-13

QUESTION: How did Elijah overcome his fear?

_____
_____
_____
_____

PRAYER FOR THE DAY: Lord, help me to listen to your voice and not my own fears as I go through my day.

DAY 2 PHILIPPIANS 4:13

QUESTION: How does relying on God help you to overcome your fear?

_____
_____
_____
_____

PRAYER FOR THE DAY: Lord, help me to trust you to give me the strength to face my fears.

WEEK 7

**U2 L2
Guts and Glory**

DAY 3 PROVERBS 29:25

QUESTION: Why should you not fear what others think of you?

_____
_____
_____
_____

PRAYER FOR THE DAY: Lord, help me to trust in YOU and not in my own strength today.

DAY 4 JOHN 14:1

QUESTION: When your day is not going well, what should you do?

_____
_____
_____
_____

PRAYER FOR THE DAY: Lord, help me to keep my focus on you today.

DAY 5 PROVERBS 17:22

QUESTION: Why should you choose to be cheerful?

_____
_____
_____
_____

PRAYER FOR THE DAY: Lord, help me to be cheerful throughout my day.

DEALING WITH FEAR

WEEK 7

U2 L2
Guts and Glory

DAY 6 PSALM 34:4

QUESTION: What fears have you overcome this week by trusting in God?

_____
_____
_____
_____

PRAYER FOR THE DAY: Lord, thank you for helping me overcome my fear of _____.

DAY 7 PSALM 9:10

QUESTION: What promise does God give when you trust in him?

_____
_____
_____
_____

PRAYER FOR THE DAY: Lord, thank you that I am never alone and that I can trust in you!

WEEKLY CHALLENGE
(WRITE YOUR WEEKLY CHALLENGE AND HOW YOU FULFILLED IT.)

DEALING WITH FEAR

U2 L2
Guts and Glory

CONVICTION

MEMORY VERSE: Judges 5:31

"So may all your enemies perish, O LORD! But may they who love you be like the sun when it rises in its strength."

DAY 1 ACTS 4:16-20

QUESTION: How did Peter and John stand up for their convictions?

_____
_____
_____
_____

PRAYER FOR THE DAY: Lord, help me to remember my convictions and to stand up for them.

DAY 2 ACTS 5:17-21

QUESTION: How were Peter and John courageous?

_____
_____
_____
_____

PRAYER FOR THE DAY: Lord, help me to be courageous in all my actions today.

**U2 L3
Guts and Glory**

DAY 3 1 CORINTHIANS 3:16-17

QUESTION: How would having the conviction that your body is God's temple affect your everyday life?

_____
_____
_____
_____

PRAYER FOR THE DAY: Lord, help me to be pure in my thoughts and actions at school today.

DAY 4 ACTS 2:45

QUESTION: How would having the conviction that we should meet each other's needs affect you today?

_____
_____
_____
_____

PRAYER FOR THE DAY: Lord, help me to think about others' needs today before my own.

DAY 5 ACTS 7:30-36

QUESTION: Moses' conviction to obey God led him to do great things. How will you obey God today?

_____
_____
_____
_____

PRAYER FOR THE DAY: Lord, help me to obey you and to do one great thing for you today.

CONVICTION

WEEK 8

U2 L3
Guts and Glory

DAY 6 ACTS 7:55-59

QUESTION: How did Stephen face death? How should you face the difficult challenges in your life today?

_____
_____
_____
_____

PRAYER FOR THE DAY: Lord, help me to stand strong in the face of any obstacles I encounter today.

DAY 7 GALATIANS 5:14-15

QUESTION: How can this passage help you to build a conviction about your relationships with others?

_____
_____
_____
_____

PRAYER FOR THE DAY: Lord, help me to love those around me and serve them with all of my heart.

WEEKLY CHALLENGE
(WRITE YOUR WEEKLY CHALLENGE AND HOW YOU FULFILLED IT.)

CONVICTION

U2 L3
Guts and Glory

AGAINST THE CROWD

MEMORY VERSE: Numbers 14:24

"But because my servant Caleb has a different spirit and follows me wholeheartedly, I will bring him into the land he went to, and his descendants will inherit it."

DAY 1 NUMBERS 14:4, 23-24

QUESTION: How did Caleb stand up to peer pressure?

_____
_____
_____
_____

PRAYER FOR THE DAY: Lord, help me to stand with you against the crowd during this week—even if I stand alone.

DAY 2 JOSHUA 14:6-9

QUESTION: Why did God reward Caleb?

_____
_____
_____
_____

PRAYER FOR THE DAY: Lord, teach me to do everything wholeheartedly.

WEEK 9

U2 L4
Guts and Glory

DAY 3 2 TIMOTHY 4:16-18

QUESTION: If everyone else deserts you, on whom should you continue to rely?

_____
_____
_____
_____

PRAYER FOR THE DAY: Lord, help me to always know that you are with me.

DAY 4 LUKE 14:16-2

QUESTION: What excuses have you made this week, or in the past, for not doing what was right?

_____
_____
_____
_____

PRAYER FOR THE DAY: Lord, thank you for helping me not to make excuses when faced with a challenge.

DAY 5 ACTS 4:13

QUESTION: How did the priests recognize that Peter and John had "been with Jesus"?

_____
_____
_____
_____

PRAYER FOR THE DAY: Lord, help me to be the kind of person who reminds people of Jesus.

AGAINST THE CROWD

WEEK 9

U2 L4
Guts and Glory

DAY 6 MATTHEW 26:36-39

QUESTION: When Jesus was afraid, where did he find strength?

_____
_____
_____
_____

PRAYER FOR THE DAY: Lord, help me to always come to you for the strength to do what is right.

DAY 7 COLOSSIANS 3:17

QUESTION: What are several things that you need to be thankful for this week?

_____
_____
_____
_____

PRAYER FOR THE DAY: Lord, help me to have a thankful heart in all that I do.

WEEKLY CHALLENGE
(WRITE YOUR WEEKLY CHALLENGE AND HOW YOU FULFILLED IT.)

AGAINST THE CROWD

WEEK 9

U2 L4
Guts and Glory

HELPING ONE ANOTHER

MEMORY VERSE: Romans 12:21

Do not be overcome by evil, but overcome evil with good.

DAY 1 1 SAMUEL 14:6-7

QUESTION: How were Jonathan and his armor-bearer courageous?

_____
_____
_____
_____

PRAYER FOR THE DAY: Lord, help me to think things through and act courageously for you today.

DAY 2 ROMANS 12:20-21

QUESTION: How can you overcome evil with good today?

_____
_____
_____
_____

PRAYER FOR THE DAY: Lord, help me to do good to others, no matter who they are.

WEEK 10

**U2 L5
Guts and Glory**

DAY 3 PROVERBS 11:16

QUESTION: Why is respect greater than wealth?
_____
_____
_____
_____

PRAYER FOR THE DAY: Lord, help me to be someone who is worthy of respect.

DAY 4 1 CORINTHIANS 16:13

QUESTION: How are courage and love related to each other?
_____
_____
_____
_____

PRAYER FOR THE DAY: Lord, teach me today to do everything in love.

DAY 5 DEUTERONOMY 31:3-6

QUESTION: In what situations do you feel afraid?
_____
_____
_____
_____

PRAYER FOR THE DAY: Lord, thank you for standing by me at all times.

HELPING ONE ANOTHER

WEEK 10

**U2 L5
Guts and Glory**

DAY 6 ACTS 23:11

QUESTION: In what situations do *you* need to take courage?
_____
_____
_____
_____

PRAYER FOR THE DAY: Lord, help me to be strong and courageous when I take your message with me today.

DAY 7 ACTS 4:13

QUESTION: What are some ways you show courage in your life?
_____
_____
_____
_____

PRAYER FOR THE DAY: Lord, help me be courageous and bring glory to your name.

WEEKLY CHALLENGE
(WRITE YOUR WEEKLY CHALLENGE AND HOW YOU FULFILLED IT.)

HELPING ONE ANOTHER

**U2 L5
Guts and Glory**

THE HUMILITY OF JESUS

MEMORY VERSE: Philippians 2:3-4

Do nothing out of selfish ambition or vain conceit, but in humility consider others better than yourselves. Each of you should look not only to your own interests, but also to the interests of others.

DAY 1 EPHESIANS 6:7-8

QUESTION: How can you serve with your whole heart today?

_____
_____
_____
_____

PRAYER FOR THE DAY: Lord, help me to do everything excellently today.

DAY 2 LUKE 16:13-15

QUESTION: Who does God expect you to serve?

_____
_____
_____
_____

PRAYER FOR THE DAY: Lord, I want to serve *you* today and not serve my desires for other things. Help me to love people today.

U3 L1
The Character of Jesus

DAY 3 MATTHEW 20:25-28

QUESTION: Are you willing to be great in God's eyes rather than in the eyes of the world?

_____
_____
_____
_____

PRAYER FOR THE DAY: Lord, help me to see all the things that I can do today to serve others.

DAY 4 2 TIMOTHY 2:24

QUESTION: Do you argue with people to get your own way?

_____
_____
_____
_____

PRAYER FOR THE DAY: Lord, please teach me to love people more and to be patient when I speak.

DAY 5 COLOSSIANS 3:23-24

QUESTION: Do you always do your best at home and at school?

_____
_____
_____
_____

PRAYER FOR THE DAY: Lord, when I am called to do something by my parents or teachers today, please help me to do it excellently for you.

THE HUMILITY OF JESUS

WEEK 11

U3 L1
The Character of Jesus

DAY 6 MATTHEW 4:8-11

QUESTION: Do you think about serving God during the day?
_____
_____
_____
_____

PRAYER FOR THE DAY: Lord, help me to remember you when I am tempted to please myself today.

DAY 7 PSALM 139:11-12

QUESTION: Do you realize that God pays attention to every decision you make?
_____
_____
_____
_____

PRAYER FOR THE DAY: Lord, when I am tempted to think that some sin does not matter to you, let me remember that you are watching.

WEEKLY CHALLENGE
(WRITE YOUR WEEKLY CHALLENGE AND HOW YOU FULFILLED IT.)

THE HUMILITY OF JESUS

**U3 L1
The Character of Jesus**

THE CONVICTION OF JESUS

MEMORY VERSE: Psalm 69:9

Zeal for your house consumes me.

DAY 1 NUMBERS 25:10

QUESTION: How did Phineas feel about God?

_____
_____
_____
_____

PRAYER FOR THE DAY: Lord, help me to have zeal and conviction about what is right, both in my own life and in the lives of those around me.

DAY 2 PROVERBS 23:17-18

QUESTION: How are you tempted to envy sinners (those who do not obey God's word)?

_____
_____
_____
_____

PRAYER FOR THE DAY: Lord, help me to hope in you and to not envy sinners.

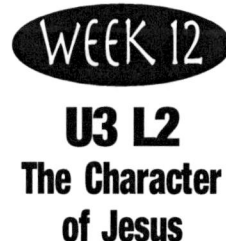

WEEK 12

**U3 L2
The Character
of Jesus**

DAY 3 ISAIAH 42:13

QUESTION: Jesus knew that God is always victorious. How can you be strong with God today?

_____
_____
_____
_____

PRAYER FOR THE DAY: Lord, give me strength today to show you and others that I love you.

DAY 4 ROMANS 12:11

QUESTION: How can being a servant keep you zealous for God?

_____
_____
_____
_____

PRAYER FOR THE DAY: Lord, help me to be like Jesus and to take opportunities to serve you by serving others.

DAY 5 I KINGS 19:10

Question: How have you been zealous for God this week?

_____
_____
_____
_____

PRAYER FOR THE DAY: I praise you, God, that you are a mighty and awesome God!

THE CONVICTION OF JESUS

WEEK 12

**U3 L2
The Character
of Jesus**

DAY 6 ROMANS 10:4

QUESTION: What is righteousness?

_____
_____
_____
_____

PRAYER FOR THE DAY: Lord, help me to always use your word as my guide.

DAY 7 ISAIAH 37:32

QUESTION: What can God's zeal accomplish in your life?

_____
_____
_____
_____

PRAYER FOR THE DAY: Lord, thank you for the way you zealously seek a relationship with me.

WEEKLY CHALLENGE
(WRITE YOUR WEEKLY CHALLENGE AND HOW YOU FULFILLED IT.)

THE CONVICTION OF JESUS

U3 L2
The Character of Jesus

THE JOY OF JESUS

MEMORY VERSE: Mark 10:15

"I tell you the truth, anyone who will not receive the kingdom of God like a little child will never enter it."

DAY 1 JOHN 15:11

QUESTION: Are you completely joyful?
___
___
___
___

PRAYER FOR THE DAY: Lord, thank you for your promise of complete joy!

DAY 2 1 JOHN 2:10

QUESTION: Do you hate anyone?
___
___
___
___

PRAYER FOR THE DAY: Lord, help me to show brotherly love toward others and to not hate anyone.

WEEK 13

**U3 L3
The Character of Jesus**

DAY 3 1 JOHN 3:18

QUESTION: Can others see your love and kindness?

_____
_____
_____
_____

PRAYER FOR THE DAY: Lord, help me to love with actions and not just with words today.

DAY 4 PSALM 118:15

QUESTION: What victories has the Lord blessed you with?

_____
_____
_____
_____

PRAYER FOR THE DAY: Lord, thank you for the many victories in my life!

DAY 5 NEHEMIAH 8:10

QUESTION: Are you happy and generous with the blessings God has given you?

_____
_____
_____
_____

PRAYER FOR THE DAY: Lord, help me to be strong because you give me great joy!

THE JOY OF JESUS

WEEK 13

**U3 L3
The Character of Jesus**

DAY 6 PROVERBS 17:22

QUESTION: Are you a cheerful person all day?

_____
_____
_____
_____

PRAYER FOR THE DAY: Lord, help me to be cheerful and happy today.

DAY 7 JOHN 13:34

QUESTION: How does Jesus tell us to love one another? Do you love those around you, and can they tell that you do?

_____
_____
_____
_____

PRAYER FOR THE DAY: Lord, help me to love others as you have loved me.

WEEKLY CHALLENGE
(WRITE YOUR WEEKLY CHALLENGE AND HOW YOU FULFILLED IT.)

THE JOY OF JESUS

**U3 L3
The Character of Jesus**

MAKING DISCIPLES

MEMORY VERSE: John 15:16

"You did not choose me, but I chose you and appointed you to go and bear fruit—fruit that will last. Then the Father will give you whatever you ask in my name."

DAY 1 JOHN 15:13

QUESTION: How have you helped a friend at school to know Jesus?

_____
_____
_____
_____

PRAYER FOR THE DAY: God, help me to show my friends at school who you really are.

DAY 2 COLOSSIANS 3:13

QUESTION: Has anyone hurt you recently? Have you forgiven that person?

_____
_____
_____
_____

PRAYER FOR THE DAY: God, help me to be as forgiving toward everyone as you are.

WEEK 14

**U4 L1
The Great Commission**

DAY 3 ROMANS 1:16-17

QUESTION: Are you ashamed of the gospel, or do you truly believe that it is God's power to save us?

___
___
___
___

PRAYER FOR THE DAY: God, please teach me not be ashamed to share your word, but to be excited to share the great news!

DAY 4 EPHESIANS 4:29-32

QUESTION: Do your actions show the world that you are trying to be like Jesus?

___
___
___
___

PRAYER FOR THE DAY: God, help my life to be a great example to those around me today.

DAY 5 COLOSSIANS 3:20

QUESTION: Do your friends see your obedience and respect for your parents?

___
___
___
___

PRAYER FOR THE DAY: God, help my family to become a light to other families in our neighborhood.

MAKING DISCIPLES

WEEK 14

**U4 L1
The Great Commission**

DAY 6 COLOSSIANS 3:12

QUESTION: Are you compassionate and caring to those around you? What does this show them?

_____
_____
_____
_____

PRAYER FOR THE DAY: God, help me to have a heart that is open and that cares for other people.

DAY 7 ACTS 17:20

QUESTION: To some people, the message of Jesus may sound strange. Does this keep you from sharing with them, or do you persevere?

_____
_____
_____
_____

PRAYER FOR THE DAY: God, please help me not to be discouraged by those who do not seem to want to know you.

WEEKLY CHALLENGE
(WRITE YOUR WEEKLY CHALLENGE AND HOW YOU FULFILLED IT.)

MAKING DISCIPLES

U4 L1
The Great Commission

ENTRUST TO RELIABLE MEN

MEMORY VERSE: Acts 8:4

Those who had been scattered preached the word wherever they went.

DAY 1 PSALM 145:13

QUESTION: Do you always keep your promises in the same way that God does?

_____
_____
_____
_____

PRAYER FOR THE DAY: God, make me a reliable person in keeping all of my promises.

DAY 2 GENESIS 39:5-6

QUESTION: How do you think Joseph treated Potiphar's things once he was entrusted with them?

_____
_____
_____
_____

PRAYER FOR THE DAY: God, help me to be more respectful when my friends trust me to take care of their things.

WEEK 15

**U4 L2
The Great
Commission**

DAY 3 1 SAMUEL 29:6

QUESTION: What is something that you can change to be as reliable as David was to Achish?

_____
_____
_____
_____

PRAYER FOR THE DAY: God, please help me to be a more reliable person toward my parents and my teachers.

DAY 4 DANIEL 6:1-3

QUESTION: What do you think motivated Daniel to be such an exceptional administrator?

_____
_____
_____
_____

PRAYER FOR THE DAY: God, help me to be an exceptional servant to my family today.

DAY 5 MATTHEW 25:22-23

Question: How do you think God feels when you are lazy?

_____
_____
_____
_____

PRAYER FOR THE DAY: God, take away my laziness. Help me to use all of the talents you have given me to your glory.

ENTRUST TO RELIABLE MEN

WEEK 15

**U4 L2
The Great Commission**

DAY 6 MATTHEW 28:18-20

QUESTION: Is making disciples of all nations an important thing to you? Why?

_____
_____
_____
_____

PRAYER FOR THE DAY: God, teach me to go after making disciples and building great relationships with all kinds of people.

DAY 7 1 CORINTHIANS 9:16-17

QUESTION: How did Paul feel about preaching the gospel that was entrusted to him? Do you feel the same way?

_____
_____
_____
_____

PRAYER FOR THE DAY: God, give me a heart that is always committed to teaching others about you.

WEEKLY CHALLENGE
(WRITE YOUR WEEKLY CHALLENGE AND HOW YOU FULFILLED IT.)

ENTRUST TO RELIABLE MEN

**U4 L2
The Great Commission**

WHATEVER THE COST

MEMORY VERSE: 2 Corinthians 8:9

For you know the grace of our Lord Jesus Christ, that though he was rich, yet for your sakes he became poor, so that you through his poverty might become rich.

DAY 1 PHILIPPIANS 2:3-8

QUESTION: Why was Jesus willing to die on the cross for us?

_____
_____
_____
_____

PRAYER FOR THE DAY: God, please help me to be grateful that Jesus was willing to sacrifice his life so that I could have a relationship with you.

DAY 2 ROMANS 12:1

QUESTION: Just as Jesus was willing to give his life for others, how can you use your life today to serve others?

_____
_____
_____
_____

PRAYER FOR THE DAY: God, please help me to love and to serve other people today.

WEEK 16

U4 L3
The Great Commission

DAY 3 GENESIS 22:1-2, 9-12

QUESTION: Why was Abraham so willing to sacrifice his only son?

___

PRAYER FOR THE DAY: God, please help me to give up things that are more important to me than you are.

DAY 4 2 CORINTHIANS 8:3-4

QUESTION: How should you feel when you give to others?

___

PRAYER FOR THE DAY: God, please help me to be excited and joyful whenever I give to others.

DAY 5 EPHESIANS 6:1-3

QUESTION: Why do you think God wants you to listen to and obey your parents, even when you don't want to?

___

PRAYER FOR THE DAY: God, help me to always understand and remember the sacrifices that my parents make for me.

WHATEVER THE COST

WEEK 16

**U4 L3
The Great Commission**

DAY 6 HEBREWS 13:15-16

QUESTION: How does God feel when we praise him and give joyfully to others?

_____
_____
_____
_____

PRAYER FOR THE DAY: God, please help me to want to please you today by praising you and giving to others.

DAY 7 MARK 12:41-44

QUESTION: Why was Jesus so impressed with this woman's sacrifice?

_____
_____
_____
_____

PRAYER FOR THE DAY: God, please let me be willing to give all that I have for you and for your glory.

WEEKLY CHALLENGE
(WRITE YOUR WEEKLY CHALLENGE AND HOW YOU FULFILLED IT.)

WHATEVER THE COST

U4 L3
The Great Commission

HE IS GOD

MEMORY VERSE: John 1:1

In the beginning was the Word, and the Word was with God, and the Word was God.

DAY 1 JOHN 1:1-5

QUESTION: What are some amazing qualities of Jesus that you can learn from this passage?

_____
_____
_____
_____

PRAYER FOR DAY: God, I am in awe of Jesus! He is our light, our truth, our example of you! There is no one else like him. Thank you for him!

DAY 2 JOHN 1:1, 2, 18

QUESTION: What do you think it was like for Jesus to be with God in heaven? What was it like for him to leave heaven and come to earth?

_____
_____
_____
_____

PRAYER FOR THE DAY: Thank you, Jesus, for leaving heaven and coming to earth to reach me!

WEEK 17

U5 L1
The Uniqueness of Jesus

DAY 3 PHILIPPIANS 2:5-11

QUESTION: Why did God exalt (lift up) Jesus?

_____
_____
_____
_____

PRAYER FOR THE DAY: God, help me to lift Jesus up in my life by being loving and sacrificial the way he was.

DAY 4 JOHN 5:30

QUESTION: Why does Jesus strive to please God?

_____
_____
_____
_____

PRAYER FOR THE DAY: God, help me to learn from Jesus how to please you every day.

DAY 5 JOHN 1:12-13

QUESTION: What is in store for those who believe in his name?

_____
_____
_____
_____

PRAYER FOR THE DAY: Thank you, Jesus, for giving me the right to become God's child.

HE IS GOD

WEEK 17

U5 L1
The Uniqueness of Jesus

DAY 6 PSALM 66:1-5

QUESTION: Why does God do his awesome deeds? What are some awesome deeds God has done in your life?
_____
_____
_____
_____

PRAYER FOR THE DAY: God, thank you so much for all you have done on my behalf!

DAY 7 JOHN 1:19-23

QUESTION: How did John the Baptist feel about Jesus?
_____
_____
_____
_____

PRAYER FOR THE DAY: God, I want to be a voice for Jesus. Help me to be like John the Baptist who pointed the way to you today.

WEEKLY CHALLENGE
(WRITE YOUR WEEKLY CHALLENGE AND HOW YOU FULFILLED IT.)

HE IS GOD

HE IS CREATOR

MEMORY VERSE: Colossians 1:16a

For by him all things were created: things in heaven and on earth.

DAY 1 PSALM 148

QUESTION: What in all of creation helps you see Jesus most clearly?

_____
_____
_____
_____

PRAYER FOR THE DAY: Jesus, I am so thankful for your creation! Thank you for drawing me close to your heart.

DAY 2 JOB 38:8-11

QUESTION: Is there anything/anyone more powerful or knowing than God and Jesus? How do you feel knowing Jesus wants to have a relationship with you?

_____
_____
_____
_____

PRAYER FOR THE DAY: God, I need to be more humble and obedient to you each day. Help me to remember that you are God and I am not!

WEEK 18

**U5 L2
The Uniqueness
of Jesus**

DAY 3 ACTS 17:24-28

QUESTION: What would it be like to have control over where lightning bolts go? To have them report to you, and say "Here we are," or to be able to give wisdom to someone?

_____
_____
_____
_____

PRAYER FOR THE DAY: God, thank you for helping me to better understand your power. Thank you for giving me my mind so that I can play, learn and love.

DAY 4 COLOSSIANS 1:18-20

QUESTION: List all the ways that Jesus is described in this passage.

_____
_____
_____
_____

PRAYER FOR THE DAY: Jesus, I want to understand who you are more and more each day!

DAY 5 PSALM 139:7-10

QUESTION: Could you hide from God? Why would you want to?

_____
_____
_____
_____

PRAYER FOR THE DAY: God, help me to remember you are beside me to guide me through each day.

HE IS CREATOR

**U5 L2
The Uniqueness of Jesus**

DAY 6 ROMANS 1:18-20

QUESTION: Why are men without excuse?
_____
_____
_____
_____

PRAYER FOR THE DAY: God, you are plain to me! Help me to grow daily in my convictions that you exist and can be clearly seen in your creation.

DAY 7 JEREMIAH 29:11-13

QUESTION: How does Jesus, the Creator, help us know God has great plans for us and loves us?
_____
_____
_____
_____

PRAYER FOR THE DAY: God, thank you for giving me hope and love each new day and for giving me Jesus to help me to understand this.

WEEKLY CHALLENGE
(WRITE YOUR WEEKLY CHALLENGE AND HOW YOU FULFILLED IT.)

HE IS CREATOR

U5 L2
The Uniqueness of Jesus

HE IS JUDGE

MEMORY VERSE: John 12:48

"There is a judge for the one who rejects me and does not accept my words; that very word which I spoke will condemn him at the last day."

DAY 1 JOHN 12:48-50

QUESTION: Why is it important to understand that the words of Jesus will judge us?

_____
_____
_____
_____

PRAYER FOR THE DAY: Jesus, thank you that your words show us clearly how to be obedient to you.

DAY 2 HEBREWS 4:12-13

QUESTION: How is God's word living and active?

_____
_____
_____
_____

PRAYER FOR THE DAY: God, thank you that nothing is hidden from you so that you can show us right and wrong every day!

**U5 L3
The Uniqueness of Jesus**

DAY 3 PSALM 139:1-4

QUESTION: How does understanding that God knows what you are going through help you to be more victorious?

_____
_____
_____
_____

PRAYER FOR DAY: God, I am so thankful that you know me so well! I look forward to being victorious over _____ today with your help.

DAY 4 PSALM 139:23-24

QUESTION: Is there anything in your life that you know offends God? What can you do to change?

_____
_____
_____
_____

PRAYER FOR THE DAY: God, please help me to be eager for correction and discipline. I know that I am loved!

DAY 5 1 SAMUEL 16:7

QUESTION: What is God's greatest concern about us?

_____
_____
_____
_____

PRAYER FOR THE DAY: Father, it is so exciting that you look at my heart and not my appearance. Help me to be eager for you to see what's in my heart each day!

HE IS JUDGE

WEEK 19

U5 L3
The Uniqueness of Jesus

DAY 6 2 TIMOTHY 4:6-8

QUESTION: Have you ever felt like giving up? How does knowing that God has the greatest reward you could ever imagine waiting for you at the end of your life encourage you to press on?

_____
_____
_____
_____

PRAYER FOR THE DAY: God, thank you that you don't let me "run" by myself. Whenever I get discouraged, please help me to remember your word and how much you love me.

DAY 7 HEBREWS 12:7-11

QUESTION: How does God discipline us? Why does God give us people who teach and train us? Who does this in your life?

_____
_____
_____
_____

PRAYER FOR THE DAY: Thank you for teaching and training me so that I can be with you forever.

WEEKLY CHALLENGE

(WRITE YOUR WEEKLY CHALLENGE AND HOW YOU FULFILLED IT.)

HE IS JUDGE

**U5 L3
The Uniqueness of Jesus**

HE IS HUMAN

MEMORY VERSE: Hebrews 4:15

For we do not have a high priest who is unable to sympathize with our weaknesses, but we have one who has been tempted in every way, just as we are—yet was without sin.

DAY 1 HEBREWS 4:14-15

QUESTION: The passage says that Jesus was like us in every way. What does that mean Jesus was like when he was a baby? A little boy? A preteen?

_____
_____
_____
_____

PRAYER FOR THE DAY: Thank you, God, for sending Jesus and making him like us so that he could help us. I will let you help me with my temptations today!

DAY 2 LUKE 2:41-52

QUESTION: Just like you, Jesus was a young child and had parents who cared for him. How would your parents have responded in the same situation? What does that tell you?

_____
_____
_____
_____

PRAYER FOR THE DAY: Lord, I am so grateful for my parents. Help me to obey them, just as Jesus obeyed his parents.

WEEK 20

**U5 L4
The Uniqueness
of Jesus**

DAY 3 MATTHEW 13:55-56

QUESTION: Be a detective. From this passage, figure out how many brothers and sisters Jesus had. How do you think Jesus treated them?

_____
_____
_____

PRAYER FOR THE DAY: Father, thank you for my brothers and sisters. Help me to treat them as Jesus would. It is a privilege to have my brothers and sisters.

DAY 4 JOHN 4:4-8

QUESTION: Look back at the quiet time from Day 1 this week. Jesus was like us in every way. How did Jesus act when he was tired, thirsty and hungry?

_____
_____
_____

PRAYER FOR THE DAY: Father, help me to think of others even when I'm tired, hungry or thirsty just as Jesus did.

DAY 5 JOHN 13:23-25

QUESTION: John was Jesus' best friend on earth. He was the one sitting close to Jesus in this passage. Who is your best friend? What special things do you do together?

_____
_____
_____

PRAYER FOR THE DAY: Thank you for my best friend. It is so awesome that you care about my life and give me friends.

HE IS HUMAN

WEEK 20

U5 L4
The Uniqueness of Jesus

DAY 6 JOHN 13:21-27

QUESTION: Jesus knew Judas was going to betray him, yet he treated him as good friend. How do you treat people who treat you badly?

_____
_____
_____
_____

PRAYER FOR THE DAY: Thank you, Father, that though I mess up, you still love me.

DAY 7 MATTHEW 26:36-46

QUESTION: Was it easy for Jesus to know he was going to die? He struggled, yet chose to do God's will.

_____
_____
_____
_____

PRAYER FOR THE DAY: Thank you that even though it was hard for him, Jesus chose to die for me.

WEEKLY CHALLENGE
(WRITE YOUR WEEKLY CHALLENGE AND HOW YOU FULFILLED IT.)

HE IS HUMAN

WEEK 20

**U5 L4
The Uniqueness of Jesus**

DISCIPLINE

MEMORY VERSE: Proverbs 14:23

All hard work brings a profit,
but mere talk leads only to poverty.

DAY 1 HEBREWS 6:10-12

QUESTION: Why does it please God when we work hard to help others?

_____
_____
_____
_____

PRAYER FOR THE DAY: God, help me to have a heart to help others today.

DAY 2 PROVERBS 6:9-11

QUESTION: Do your parents have to wake you up in the morning? Why should you get up on your own?

_____
_____
_____
_____

PRAYER FOR THE DAY: God, help me not be lazy, but to get up early to have time with you.

U6 L1
Proverbs

DAY 3 MARK 1:35

QUESTION: Why did Jesus get up early to pray?
_____
_____
_____

PRAYER FOR THE DAY: God, help me to start my day praying and studying my Bible.

DAY 4 PROVERBS 10:4

QUESTION: Do you want to be poor or wealthy? Why does hard work bring wealth and laziness bring poverty?
_____
_____
_____

PRAYER FOR THE DAY: God, help me to work hard at home and at school.

DAY 5 PROVERBS 13:4

QUESTION: Why does the lazy man get nothing while the diligent man is satisfied?
_____
_____
_____

PRAYER FOR THE DAY: God, help me to work diligently in everything I do today. Thank you for the rewards that hard work brings.

DISCIPLINE

WEEK 21

U6 L1
Proverbs

DAY 6 2 TIMOTHY 1:7

QUESTION: In what areas do you need to be self-disciplined?
_____
_____
_____
_____

PRAYER FOR THE DAY: God, help me to be disciplined in _____ today.

DAY 7 1 THESSALONIANS 5:12-13

QUESTION: Who do you know in your church who works hard? Why should you respect them?
_____
_____
_____
_____

PRAYER FOR THE DAY: God, help me to respect the people who work hard and imitate their example today.

WEEKLY CHALLENGE
(WRITE YOUR WEEKLY CHALLENGE AND HOW YOU FULFILLED IT.)

DISCIPLINE

U6 L1
Proverbs

SPEECH

MEMORY VERSE: Proverbs 16:24

Pleasant words are a honeycomb,
sweet to the soul and healing to the bones.

DAY 1 PROVERBS 25:11

QUESTION: What does the dictionary say "aptly" means? How valuable is good speech?

_____
_____
_____
_____

PRAYER FOR THE DAY: God, help me to choose my words carefully throughout the day.

DAY 2 PROVERBS 18:13

QUESTION: How do I feel when someone interrupts me?

_____
_____
_____
_____

PRAYER FOR THE DAY: God, help me to listen to others and to not interrupt them today.

WEEK 22

**U6 L2
Proverbs**

DAY 3 PROVERBS 15:1

QUESTION: Can one person stop a fight?

_____
_____
_____
_____

PRAYER FOR THE DAY: God, help me to be a person who speaks kindly, even if others do not.

DAY 4 PROVERBS 13:3

QUESTION: What does it mean to speak "rashly"? How does my speech sometimes get me into trouble?

_____
_____
_____
_____

PRAYER FOR THE DAY: God, help me to think before I speak today.

DAY 5 PROVERBS 20:19

QUESTION: Why is it hard to trust someone who gossips to you about others?

_____
_____
_____
_____

PRAYER FOR THE DAY: God, help me not to gossip or to listen to gossip.

SPEECH

WEEK 22

U6 L2
Proverbs

DAY 6 PROVERBS 18:2

QUESTION: How do you feel around someone who seems to never stop talking?

_____
_____
_____
_____

PRAYER FOR THE DAY: God, help me to be a good listener today.

DAY 7 JAMES 3:9-12

QUESTION: How do I use my tongue daily—to praise God or to hurt others?

_____
_____
_____
_____

PRAYER FOR THE DAY: God, please help me today to use my tongue to praise you and to build others up.

WEEKLY CHALLENGE
(WRITE YOUR WEEKLY CHALLENGE AND HOW YOU FULFILLED IT.)

SPEECH

WEEK 22

U6 L2
Proverbs

LIVING WISELY

MEMORY VERSE: Proverbs 19:20

Listen to advice and accept instruction
and in the end you will be wise.

DAY 1 PROVERBS 12:15

QUESTION: In what way will you listen to advice today?
_____
_____
_____
_____

PRAYER FOR THE DAY: God, when I am given advice that is for my own good, help me to take it with a great attitude.

DAY 2 PROVERBS 13:10

QUESTION: When you were in a situation where you did not agree with someone, did you seek advice before dealing with it?
_____
_____
_____
_____

PRAYER FOR THE DAY: God, help me to seek advice when I have disagreements with others.

WEEK 23

U6 L3
Proverbs

DAY 3 PROVERBS 16:16

QUESTION: Why is it better to get wisdom than to get gold?

_____
_____
_____
_____

PRAYER FOR THE DAY: God, please help me to remember that knowing you is more important than getting more things.

DAY 4 COLOSSIANS 2:2-3

QUESTION: Where does wisdom ultimately come from?

_____
_____
_____
_____

PRAYER FOR THE DAY: Father, help me to seek advice from those who know me well.

DAY 5 ECCLESIASTES 7:19

QUESTION: Why does being wise make you more powerful than ten rulers?

_____
_____
_____
_____

PRAYER FOR THE DAY: God, help me to always see how important wisdom is.

LIVING WISELY

WEEK 23

**U6 L3
Proverbs**

DAY 6 LUKE 21:15

Question: Do you believe God wants you to be wise?
_____
_____
_____
_____

Prayer for the day: God, give me the words of wisdom to handle correctly those who are not kind to me today.

DAY 7 JAMES 1:5

Question: In what ways will you trust God to give you wisdom today?
_____
_____
_____
_____

Prayer for the day: God, today and everyday, please help me to seek and accept your wisdom.

WEEKLY CHALLENGE
(WRITE YOUR WEEKLY CHALLENGE AND HOW YOU FULFILLED IT.)

LIVING WISELY

U6 L3
Proverbs

THINGS GOD HATES

MEMORY VERSE: Proverbs 6:16-19

There are six things the Lord hates,
seven that are detestable to him:
haughty eyes, a lying tongue,
hands that shed innocent blood,
a heart that devises wicked schemes,
feet that are quick to rush into evil,
a false witness who pours out lies
and a man who stirs up dissension
among his brothers.

DAY 1 PROVERBS 16:17

QUESTION: "haughty eyes" - When you are prideful, you think you know everything. How can this make you fail?

_____
_____
_____

PRAYER FOR THE DAY: God, help me to want to listen to and to learn from others.

DAY 2 PROVERBS 12:19

QUESTION: "lying tongue" - How do you feel when someone has been lying to you? How long do those friendships last?

_____
_____
_____

PRAYER FOR THE DAY: God, help me to be honest in all my friendships.

U6 L4
Proverbs

DAY 3 MATTHEW 27:4

QUESTION: "innocent blood" - Why might you accuse someone of doing something they didn't do? (Think about Jesus and why people wanted to kill him.)

_____
_____
_____
_____

PRAYER FOR THE DAY: God, help me to always take responsibility for my own sin and not to blame others.

DAY 4 PROVERBS 4:20-21

QUESTION: "heart" - What can you do to keep your heart from thinking of bad things to do?

_____
_____
_____
_____

PRAYER FOR THE DAY: God, help me to remember my scripture memory verse.

DAY 5 PROVERBS 22:3

QUESTION: "quick to do evil" - How can you keep from doing something you will feel bad about later?

_____
_____
_____
_____

PRAYER FOR THE DAY: God, help me to think before I act.

THINGS GOD HATES

**U6 L4
Proverbs**

DAY 6 PROVERBS 25:18

QUESTION: "false witness" - How can you hurt other people with your words?

_____
_____
_____
_____

PRAYER FOR THE DAY: Father, help me to always talk in a way that builds my friends up and doesn't hurt them.

DAY 7 PROVERBS 16:28

Question: "dissension" - How does gossip split up friends?

_____
_____
_____
_____

PRAYER FOR THE DAY: God, help me not to gossip about others or listen to it today.

WEEKLY CHALLENGE
(WRITE YOUR WEEKLY CHALLENGE AND HOW YOU FULFILLED IT.)

THINGS GOD HATES

U6 L4
Proverbs

MATERIALISM

MEMORY VERSE: Proverbs 11:24

One man gives freely, yet gains even more; another withholds unduly, but comes to poverty.

DAY 1 LUKE 21:1-4

QUESTION: Why was Jesus pleased with this woman who gave so little?

_____
_____
_____
_____

PRAYER FOR THE DAY: God, help me to always sacrifice for you.

DAY 2 1 TIMOTHY 6:10

QUESTION: What can happen if you love money?

_____
_____
_____
_____

PRAYER FOR THE DAY: God, help me not to let things be more important than you.

**U6 L5
Proverbs**

DAY 3 PROVERBS 13:11

QUESTION: How could you be tempted to be dishonest with money?

_____
_____
_____
_____

PRAYER FOR THE DAY: God, help me to always be honest with money.

DAY 4 PROVERBS 12:11

QUESTION: Have you ever dreamed of winning a lot of money? Why?

_____
_____
_____
_____

PRAYER FOR THE DAY: God, help me to want to work hard for my money.

DAY 5 2 CORINTHIANS 8:1-3

QUESTION: How did the churches in Macedonia encourage the early Christians?

_____
_____
_____
_____

PRAYER FOR THE DAY: God, help our preteen class to encourage our church by our giving.

MATERIALISM

WEEK 25

U6 L5
Proverbs

DAY 6 PROVERBS 27:24

QUESTION: What will happen to your things when you die?
_____
_____
_____
_____

PRAYER FOR THE DAY: God, help me to value eternal things!

DAY 7 2 CORINTHIANS 9:7

QUESTION: How should you feel when you give?
_____
_____
_____
_____

PRAYER FOR THE DAY: God, help me to be happy about my giving.

WEEKLY CHALLENGE
(WRITE YOUR WEEKLY CHALLENGE AND HOW YOU FULFILLED IT.)

MATERIALISM

WEEK 25

U6 L5
Proverbs

HUMILITY

MEMORY VERSE: Proverbs 13:10

**Pride only breeds quarrels,
   but wisdom is found in those who take advice.**

DAY 1 PROVERBS 14:12

QUESTION: Think back to a time when you were wrong. How did you feel when someone tried to point it out to you?

_____
_____
_____
_____

PRAYER FOR THE DAY: God, help me to be open to letting others be in my life.

DAY 2 PROVERBS 16:18

QUESTION: How does pride cause you to fall or fail?

_____
_____
_____
_____

PRAYER FOR THE DAY: God, help me to see how destructive pride really is.

WEEK 26

**U6 L6
Proverbs**

DAY 3 PROVERBS 28:26

QUESTION: Why do you need other people to help you? Why can't you do it all on your own?

_____
_____
_____
_____

PRAYER FOR THE DAY: God, help me to seek help from someone today about something I want to change.

DAY 4 PROVERBS 27:2

QUESTION: How does it feel to listen to someone who is boasting?

_____
_____
_____
_____

PRAYER FOR THE DAY: God, help me let others praise me instead of bragging about myself.

DAY 5 MATTHEW 20:25-26

QUESTION: How do you become great in God's eyes?

_____
_____
_____
_____

PRAYER FOR THE DAY: God, help me to imitate Jesus and to be great in your eyes today.

HUMILITY

WEEK 26

U6 L6
Proverbs

DAY 6 EPHESIANS 4:2A

QUESTION: Would those who know you say that you are humble or prideful?

_____
_____
_____
_____

PRAYER FOR THE DAY: God, please help me to be completely humble in my words and actions today.

DAY 7 PHILIPPIANS 2:3-4

QUESTION: Why is it hard to put others first?

_____
_____
_____
_____

PRAYER FOR THE DAY: God, help me not to think that I am better than anyone else.

WEEKLY CHALLENGE
(WRITE YOUR WEEKLY CHALLENGE AND HOW YOU FULFILLED IT.)

HUMILITY

WEEK 26

U6 L6
Proverbs

SPIRITUAL RELATIONSHIPS

MEMORY VERSE: Acts 4:13

When they saw the courage of Peter and John and realized that they were unschooled, ordinary men, they were astonished and they took note that these men had been with Jesus.

DAY 1 PSALM 73:28

QUESTION: Why is it good for you "to be near God"?

_____
_____
_____
_____

PRAYER FOR THE DAY: God, help me today to understand how special you are.

DAY 2 JOHN 15:5

QUESTION: Why can you do more with Jesus than you can without him?

_____
_____
_____
_____

PRAYER FOR THE DAY: God, help me to obey your word today, no matter what happens.

WEEK 27

U7 L1
Friendship

DAY 3 JOSHUA 1:8

QUESTION: Why will following the Bible make you successful in life?

_____
_____
_____
_____

PRAYER FOR THE DAY: God, help me to think about you all day long today.

DAY 4 EPHESIANS 6:10-11

QUESTION: How can you become strong in the Lord?

_____
_____
_____
_____

PRAYER FOR THE DAY: God, help me stand up to Satan today and not give into fear, anger or laziness.

DAY 5 2 TIMOTHY 1:7

QUESTION: What situations make you feel timid and shy?

_____
_____
_____
_____

PRAYER FOR THE DAY: God, help me to remember your power whenever I feel timid today.

SPIRITUAL RELATIONSHIPS

WEEK 27

**U7 L1
Friendship**

DAY 6 MATTHEW 19:26

QUESTION: What area of your life is the most challenging for you (school, parents, friends, emotions)?

_____
_____
_____
_____

PRAYER FOR THE DAY: God, help me to believe with all my heart that you can fix my problems.

DAY 7 PHILIPPIANS 4:13

QUESTION: What is the most difficult thing you will have to do today?

_____
_____
_____
_____

PRAYER FOR THE DAY: God, thank you for helping me to do great today in _____ .

WEEKLY CHALLENGE
(WRITE YOUR WEEKLY CHALLENGE AND HOW YOU FULFILLED IT.)

SPIRITUAL RELATIONSHIPS

WEEK 27

U7 L1
Friendship

PEER PRESSURE

MEMORY VERSE: Proverbs 13:20

He who walks with the wise grows wise,
but a companion of fools suffers harm.

DAY 1 PROVERBS 12:26

QUESTION: Why would a person need to be "cautious" in making new friends?

_____
_____
_____
_____

PRAYER FOR THE DAY: God, help me understand how to make good friends.

DAY 2 1 CORINTHIANS 15:33

QUESTION: Why is it so important to choose the right friends?

_____
_____
_____
_____

PRAYER FOR THE DAY: God, please give me the desire to choose the friends you want me to have.

WEEK 28

**U7 L2
Friendship**

DAY 3 1 SAMUEL 18:1

QUESTION: Who is your best friend and why?
_____
_____
_____
_____

PRAYER FOR THE DAY: God, help me to have a best friend at church.

DAY 4 PROVERBS 13:20

QUESTION: How do your friends help you do what is right?
_____
_____
_____
_____

PRAYER FOR THE DAY: God, thank you that there are people who are trying to help me to obey you.

DAY 5 1 KINGS 3:5, 9-13

QUESTION: How did Solomon's request benefit himself and other people?
_____
_____
_____
_____

PRAYER FOR THE DAY: God, please help me to make wise choices today.

PEER PRESSURE

WEEK 28

**U7 L2
Friendship**

DAY 6 1 SAMUEL 16:1, 6-7

QUESTION: What criteria does God use in choosing leaders for his kingdom?

_____
_____
_____

PRAYER FOR THE DAY: God, help me to have a heart just like yours.

DAY 7 PSALM 119:63

QUESTION: Why should your best friends be those who love and obey God?

_____
_____
_____

PRAYER FOR THE DAY: God, thank you for the wonderful relationships I can have because of you!

WEEKLY CHALLENGE
(WRITE YOUR WEEKLY CHALLENGE AND HOW YOU FULFILLED IT.)

PEER PRESSURE

U7 L2
Friendship

BEING A TEAM

MEMORY VERSE: Romans 12:5

So in Christ we who are many form one body, and each member belongs to all the others.

DAY 1 1 CORINTHIANS 12:27

QUESTION: Who are your best friends at church, and why are they special to you?

_____
_____
_____

PRAYER FOR THE DAY: God, thank you for the great friends I have in your kingdom.

DAY 2 HEBREWS 10:24

QUESTION: How can you help your friends be more loving today?

_____
_____
_____

PRAYER FOR THE DAY: God, show me three kind deeds I can do today.

**U7 L3
Friendship**

DAY 3 GALATIANS 6:2

QUESTION: How would you help a friend at church who forgot the memory verse?

_____
_____
_____
_____

PRAYER FOR THE DAY: God, please help me to see and meet the needs of my friends.

DAY 4 ROMANS 12:10

QUESTION: What can you do to serve a friend from church today?

_____
_____
_____
_____

PRAYER FOR THE DAY: God, help me to be unselfish and eager to help others today.

DAY 5 PHILIPPIANS 2:19-21

QUESTION: Do you notice when one of your classmates at church is sad or absent?

_____
_____
_____
_____

PRAYER FOR THE DAY: God, please help me to be concerned about how my friends are doing.

BEING A TEAM

WEEK 29

U7 L3
Friendship

DAY 6 EPHESIANS 6:18

QUESTION: How often do you pray for your friends at church?
_____
_____
_____
_____

PRAYER FOR THE DAY: God, help me to remember to pray for the needs of my friends, not just for my own needs.

DAY 7 PSALM 133:1

QUESTION: Why is unity a "good and pleasant" thing?
_____
_____
_____
_____

PRAYER FOR THE DAY: God, thank you for giving me such a great team to be a part of at church.

WEEKLY CHALLENGE
(WRITE YOUR WEEKLY CHALLENGE AND HOW YOU FULFILLED IT.)

BEING A TEAM

WEEK 29

**U7 L3
Friendship**

BUILDING DEEP RELATIONSHIPS

MEMORY VERSE: Philippians 2:4

Each of you should look not only to your own interests, but also to the interests of others.

DAY 1 1 JOHN 4:20-21

QUESTION: Who do you have a hard time being friends with?

_____
_____
_____
_____

PRAYER FOR THE DAY: God, please help me to love everyone around me, even those who are different from me.

DAY 2 JOHN 15:12-13

QUESTION: What do you think it means to "lay down your life" for your friends?

_____
_____
_____
_____

PRAYER FOR THE DAY: God, teach me how to give of myself to others today.

**U7 L4
Friendship**

DAY 3 EPHESIANS 4:1-2

QUESTION: In what ways are you impatient with your friends?
_____
_____
_____
_____

PRAYER FOR THE DAY: God, please show me how I can be more patient.

DAY 4 MATTHEW 26:36-38

QUESTION: Do you share your struggles with your friends? Why or why not?
_____
_____
_____
_____

PRAYER FOR THE DAY: God, help me to be more open about the way I really feel about things, starting today.

DAY 5 PROVERBS 27:17

QUESTION: How can you "sharpen" your friends as "iron sharpens iron"?
_____
_____
_____
_____

PRAYER FOR THE DAY: God, please help me to love my friends enough to challenge them when they are not doing what's right.

BUILDING DEEP RELATIONSHIPS

WEEK 30

**U7 L4
Friendship**

DAY 6 MARK 6:30-32

QUESTION: Why is it important to spend fun time with your church classmates?

_____
_____
_____
_____

PRAYER FOR THE DAY: God, thank you for the fun times you have given me with my friends.

DAY 7 PHILIPPIANS 1:3

QUESTION: What are you thankful for in your friendships?

_____
_____
_____
_____

PRAYER FOR THE DAY: God, thank you for giving me such special people for friends.

WEEKLY CHALLENGE
(WRITE YOUR WEEKLY CHALLENGE AND HOW YOU FULFILLED IT.)

BUILDING DEEP RELATIONSHIPS

WEEK 30

U7 L4
Friendship

COMMUNICATION

MEMORY VERSE: Proverbs 18:13

He who answers before listening—
that is his folly and his shame.

DAY 1 MARK 1:16-20

QUESTION: How did the disciples respond when Jesus spoke to them?

_____
_____
_____
_____

PRAYER FOR THE DAY: God, please help me to follow directions the first time they are given to me.

DAY 2 PROVERBS 19:20

QUESTION: How do you feel when your parents talk to you about your behavior?

_____
_____
_____
_____

PRAYER FOR THE DAY: God, help me to be grateful that there are people who want to help me be my best.

WEEK 31

**U7 L5
Friendship**

DAY 3 JAMES 1:19

QUESTION: Who are you "quick to listen" to, and who do you ignore?

_____
_____
_____
_____

PRAYER FOR THE DAY: God, help me to give people my full attention when I am listening to them today.

DAY 4 1 TIMOTHY 4:12

QUESTION: How do you need to change in order to be a good example in the way you talk?

_____
_____
_____
_____

PRAYER FOR THE DAY: God, please give me the wisdom to know what to say and what not to say in all situations today.

DAY 5 PROVERBS 12:18

QUESTION: How can words be "reckless" and hurt someone like a sword?

_____
_____
_____
_____

PRAYER FOR THE DAY: God, please help me to always think before I speak.

COMMUNICATION

WEEK 31

**U7 L5
Friendship**

DAY 6 PROVERBS 16:28

QUESTION: Why does God hate gossip?
___
___
___
___

PRAYER FOR THE DAY: God, help me not to say unkind things about other people today.

DAY 7 EPHESIANS 4:29

QUESTION: What could you say to your best friend to make him or her spiritually stronger? When will you say it?
___
___
___
___

PRAYER FOR THE DAY: God, help me to use my words to make people stronger, not weaker.

WEEKLY CHALLENGE
(WRITE YOUR WEEKLY CHALLENGE AND HOW YOU FULFILLED IT.)

COMMUNICATION

**U7 L5
Friendship**

SAMARITAN WOMAN

MEMORY VERSE: John 4:24

> God is spirit, and his worshipers must worship in spirit and in truth.

DAY 1 LUKE 5:22-25

QUESTION: Jesus always told the truth. How do you think it affected the Pharisees and teachers that Jesus knew what they were thinking?

_____
_____
_____
_____

PRAYER FOR THE DAY: God, help me to be honest with my family and friends today.

DAY 2 LUKE 6:27-31

QUESTION: Jesus showed love to people who did not love him. If there is someone who you think doesn't like you, how can you show love to them?

_____
_____
_____
_____

PRAYER FOR THE DAY: God, help me to love others even when they don't seem to love me.

WEEK 32

**U8 L1
Changed Lives**

DAY 3 HEBREWS 4:13

QUESTION: What one thing do you want to change after reading this scripture?

_____
_____
_____
_____

PRAYER FOR THE DAY: God, help me to remember that you always know everything about me.

DAY 4 HEBREWS 13:1

QUESTION: How does Jesus treat you like you are family?

_____
_____
_____
_____

PRAYER FOR THE DAY: God, please help me to treat others like my family today.

DAY 5 1 JOHN 4:10-11

QUESTION: How do you know that God loves you?

_____
_____
_____
_____

PRAYER FOR THE DAY: God, thank you for loving me first. Help me to love others first.

SAMARITAN WOMAN

WEEK 32

U8 L1
Changed Lives

DAY 6 JOHN 7:24

QUESTION: At school today, what is a kind thing you can do for someone who is different from you?

_____
_____
_____
_____

PRAYER FOR THE DAY: God, help me to have confidence to talk to someone at school today who needs a friend.

DAY 7 JOHN 1:43-49

QUESTION: How did Jesus know that there was nothing false in Nathaniel if they had not yet met?

_____
_____
_____
_____

PRAYER FOR THE DAY: God, help me to not want to hide anything from you.

WEEKLY CHALLENGE
(WRITE YOUR WEEKLY CHALLENGE AND HOW YOU FULFILLED IT.)

SAMARITAN WOMAN

WEEK 32

U8 L1
Changed Lives

ZACCHAEUS

MEMORY VERSE: Luke 19:10

"For the Son of Man came to seek and save what was lost."

DAY 1 MATTHEW 18:2-4

QUESTION: What is something you want to change for God?
___
___
___
___

PRAYER FOR THE DAY: God, help me to be eager to change, starting today.

DAY 2 ACTS 17:10-11

QUESTION: How can you tell if a person is eager to read the Bible? Are you eager?
___
___
___
___

PRAYER FOR THE DAY: God, help me to love to read the Bible!

WEEK 33

**U8 L2
Changed Lives**

DAY 3 2 PETER 1:3-8

QUESTION: Which of the qualities listed in verses 5-7 do you feel you need more of in your life?

_____
_____
_____
_____

PRAYER FOR THE DAY: God, help me continue to grow and change in this area.

DAY 4 MARK 12:28-31

QUESTION: What are the four areas in which God wants you to give your all?

_____
_____
_____
_____

PRAYER FOR THE DAY: God, help me love people with all my heart like you do.

DAY 5 PSALM 51:12

QUESTION: Why is it important to have a willing spirit?

_____
_____
_____
_____

PRAYER FOR THE DAY: God, please grant me a willing spirit today.

ZACCHAEUS

WEEK 33

U8 L2
Changed Lives

DAY 6 2 KINGS 23:1-3, 25

QUESTION: What was the people's response?
_____
_____
_____
_____

PRAYER FOR THE DAY: God, help me give you all of my heart, soul and strength.

DAY 7 HEBREWS 13:8

QUESTION: Why is it important that Jesus doesn't change?
_____
_____
_____
_____

PRAYER FOR THE DAY: God, thank you for Jesus! I'm glad I can count on you.

WEEKLY CHALLENGE
(WRITE YOUR WEEKLY CHALLENGE AND HOW YOU FULFILLED IT.)

ZACCHAEUS

U8 L2
Changed Lives

LYDIA

MEMORY VERSE: Matthew 6:33

"But seek first his kingdom and his righteousness, and all these things will be given to you as well."

DAY 1 PSALM 18:32-35

QUESTION: How does this scripture make you feel as you begin your day?

_____
_____
_____
_____

PRAYER FOR THE DAY: God, help me to remember today that my strength and confidence come from you.

DAY 2 JOHN 15:1-5

QUESTION: Apart from God you can do nothing. What does it mean to remain in him?

_____
_____
_____
_____

PRAYER FOR THE DAY: God, please help me to stay close to you this week.

WEEK 34

**U8 L3
Changed Lives**

DAY 3 PSALM 37:4

QUESTION: What does God promise he will do if you delight in him?

_____
_____
_____
_____

PRAYER FOR THE DAY: God, help me to see how I can please you rather than please myself.

DAY 4 HAGGAI 1:7-11

QUESTION: According to verse 9, why was God holding back his blessings and allowing the people to live frustrated lives?

_____
_____
_____
_____

PRAYER FOR THE DAY: God, I pray that in all I do today, I won't crowd out my time for you and your people.

DAY 5 JEREMIAH 17:5-8

QUESTION: What are the consequences of trusting in yourself? What are the blessings if you trust in God?

_____
_____
_____
_____

PRAYER FOR THE DAY: God, please help me to rely on you today.

LYDIA

WEEK 34

U8 L3
Changed Lives

DAY 6 PROVERBS 3:5-6

QUESTION: In what ways can you lean on God's understanding and not your own?

_____
_____
_____
_____

PRAYER FOR THE DAY: God, help me to go to your word and to disciples for direction in my life.

DAY 7 MATTHEW 6:31-33

QUESTION: What kinds of things do you worry about?

_____
_____
_____
_____

PRAYER FOR THE DAY: God, help me not to worry about _____ and to trust in you.

WEEKLY CHALLENGE
(WRITE YOUR WEEKLY CHALLENGE AND HOW YOU FULFILLED IT.)

LYDIA

WEEK 34

**U8 L3
Changed Lives**

THE ETHIOPIAN

MEMORY VERSE: **Hebrews 13:7**

Remember your leaders, who spoke the word of God to you. Consider the outcome of their way of life and imitate their faith.

DAY 1 JEREMIAH 29:11

QUESTION: What plans do you think God has for you?

_____
_____
_____
_____

PRAYER FOR THE DAY: God, thank you so much for having great plans for my future.

DAY 2 ACTS 17:26-27

QUESTION: Where do you think God wants you?

_____
_____
_____
_____

PRAYER FOR THE DAY: God, help me to understand—and be happy—that I am where you want me to be.

WEEK 35

**U8 L4
Changed Lives**

DAY 3 ACTS 18:24-28

QUESTION: What is a question that you have about Jesus or the Bible?

_____
_____
_____
_____

PRAYER FOR THE DAY: God, help me to ask someone today for an explanation to that question.

DAY 4 LUKE 11:1-4

QUESTION: Why did the disciples want to know how to pray?

_____
_____
_____
_____

PRAYER FOR THE DAY: God, thank you for giving me a way to talk directly to you.

DAY 5 ACTS 16:25-34

QUESTION: Why did the jailer ask Paul and Silas about salvation?

_____
_____
_____
_____

PRAYER FOR THE DAY: God, help me to be teachable today.

THE ETHIOPIAN

WEEK 35

**U8 L4
Changed Lives**

DAY 6 JAMES 1:22-25

QUESTION: What is something you know you should do that you haven't been doing?

_____
_____
_____
_____

PRAYER FOR THE DAY: God, help me to do it today!

DAY 7 MATTHEW 28:18-20

QUESTION: Who has God put in your life to help you seek him?

_____
_____
_____
_____

PRAYER FOR THE DAY: God, help me to seek advice today.

WEEKLY CHALLENGE
(WRITE YOUR WEEKLY CHALLENGE AND HOW YOU FULFILLED IT.)

THE ETHIOPIAN

**U8 L4
Changed Lives**

THE PLAN

MEMORY VERSE: Ephesians 6:1-3

Children, obey your parents in the Lord, for this is right. Honor your father and mother—which is the first commandment with a promise—that it may go well with you and that you may enjoy long life on the earth.

DAY 1 EPHESIANS 5:25-30

QUESTION: How do you think a wife feels when her husband loves her like Jesus loves the church?

_____
_____
_____
_____

PRAYER FOR THE DAY: God, thank you for your plan for marriage.

DAY 2 EPHESIANS 5:22-23, 33

QUESTION: How do you think a husband feels when his wife submits to and respects his leadership?

_____
_____
_____
_____

PRAYER FOR THE DAY: God, please help the wives in the church to respect their husbands the way the church respects Jesus.

WEEK 36

U9 L1
Family

DAY 3 1 THESSALONIANS 2:10-11

QUESTION: Is it easy to be a father? Why or why not?

_____
_____
_____
_____

PRAYER FOR THE DAY: God, please help me to appreciate how hard the dads in the church work to be good parents.

DAY 4 1 THESSALONIANS 2:7-9

QUESTION: Is it easy to be a mother? Why or why not?

_____
_____
_____
_____

PRAYER FOR THE DAY: God, please help me to appreciate how hard the mothers in the church work to help their children.

DAY 5 LUKE 18:29-30

QUESTION: When you think of the church, who are like parents and brothers and sisters to you?

_____
_____
_____
_____

PRAYER FOR THE DAY: God, please help me to reach out to others in the church as if they were in my physical family.

THE PLAN

WEEK 36

U9 L1
Family

DAY 6 PSALM 68:5-6

QUESTION: God created families so that people would not be _____. God created the church so that people would not be _____.

_____
_____
_____
_____

PRAYER FOR THE DAY: God, thank you very much for giving me my family.

DAY 7 PSALM 68:5-6

QUESTION: What will God do for those who have no father or mother?

_____
_____
_____
_____

PRAYER FOR THE DAY: God, I am thankful that you will put them in your family.

WEEKLY CHALLENGE
(WRITE YOUR WEEKLY CHALLENGE AND HOW YOU FULFILLED IT.)

THE PLAN

U9 L1
Family

MARRIAGE

MEMORY VERSE: Ephesians 5:3

But among you there must not be even a hint of sexual immorality, or of any kind of impurity, or of greed, for these are improper for God's holy people.

DAY 1 JEREMIAH 29:11

QUESTION: Do you trust that God has a plan to bless your life?

_____
_____
_____
_____

PRAYER FOR THE DAY: God, please help me trust you with your plan of purity for my life.

DAY 2 EPHESIANS 5:22-33

QUESTION: List some couples who you think have a marriage as described in Ephesians 5.

_____
_____
_____
_____

PRAYER FOR THE DAY: God, thank you for your plan for marriage.

**U9 L2
Family**

DAY 3 1 THESSALONIANS 4:3-6

QUESTION: Would you drink polluted water? How does thinking about this help you to understand the importance of also keeping your heart pure?

_____
_____
_____
_____

PRAYER FOR THE DAY: God, please give me the heart to be completely pure in my thoughts and actions and to be pure in my relationships with girls or guys.

DAY 4 PROVERBS 1:8-9

QUESTION: Are you willing to learn, or do you think you already know the scoop on purity?

_____
_____
_____
_____

PRAYER FOR THE DAY: God, please help me to humbly learn about dating, about relationships with girls or guys, from my parents and from older disciples who are dating.

DAY 5 2 CORINTHIANS 6:14

QUESTION: When I begin to date, why should I only date disciples?

_____
_____
_____
_____

PRAYER FOR THE DAY: God, please help me get the con-viction that I will only date and marry a disciple.

MARRIAGE

WEEK 37

U9 L2
Family

DAY 6 1 TIMOTHY 5:1-2

QUESTION: When you treat someone with disrespect, who are you really disrespecting?

_____
_____
_____
_____

PRAYER FOR THE DAY: God, please help me learn to respect girls (if you are a guy) and guys (if you are a girl).

DAY 7 COLOSSIANS 3:5

QUESTION: When you were a little kid and did something wrong, you would run and hide. When we are impure, we want to hide. Are you hiding now? If so, do you like it?

_____
_____
_____
_____

PRAYER FOR THE DAY: God, please help me to hate impurity with all my heart because it destroys people and relationships.

WEEKLY CHALLENGE
(WRITE YOUR WEEKLY CHALLENGE AND HOW YOU FULFILLED IT.)

MARRIAGE

U9 L2
Family

RESPECT

MEMORY VERSE: Matthew 7:12

"So in everything, do to others what you would have them do to you, for this sums up the Law and the Prophets."

DAY 1 EPHESIANS 6:1-3

QUESTION: Why should you respect your parents? Ask your parents if they feel respected. Why do they or don't they?

_____
_____
_____

PRAYER FOR THE DAY: God, please help me listen to my parents with an open heart today.

DAY 2 JAMES 1:19-20

QUESTION: How do these specific directions help in showing respect? Pick one of the three to work on today.

_____
_____
_____

PRAYER FOR THE DAY: God, please make clear to me those areas of my character in which I show disrespect so that I can change.

WEEK 38

U9 L3
Family

DAY 3 1 THESSALONIANS 5:12-13

QUESTION: List people who are "over you" in different areas. How should you respond to correction and discipline from them?

___
___
___
___

PRAYER FOR THE DAY: God, please help me respect the authority you have put in my life today.

DAY 4 PHILIPPIANS 2:3-4

QUESTION: What are some practical ways to think of someone before yourself today? Who will that person be?

___
___
___
___

PRAYER FOR THE DAY: God, please help me serve others today.

DAY 5 EPHESIANS 4:32

QUESTIONS: Am I willing to forgive others when I have been hurt by them? How can I show forgiveness?

___
___
___
___

PRAYER FOR THE DAY: God, please help me to see that being forgiving is being respectful.

RESPECT

WEEK 38

U9 L3
Family

DAY 6 LUKE 2:51

QUESTION: Am I respecting my parents with all my heart?

_____
_____
_____
_____

PRAYER FOR THE DAY: God, please help me respect my parents as Jesus respected his.

DAY 7 MATTHEW 7:12

QUESTION: How would I feel if others showed me the respect that I show to them?

_____
_____
_____
_____

PRAYER FOR THE DAY: God, please help me to treat everyone with the same respect that I would like to receive.

WEEKLY CHALLENGE
(WRITE YOUR WEEKLY CHALLENGE AND HOW YOU FULFILLED IT.)

RESPECT

WEEK 38

U9 L3
Family

RESOLVING CONFLICT

MEMORY VERSE: Ephesians 4:26-27

In your anger do not sin: Do not let the sun go down while you are still angry, and do not give the devil a foothold.

DAY 1 EPHESIANS 4:26

QUESTION: Can you think of someone with whom you have an unresolved conflict?

___
___
___
___

PRAYER FOR THE DAY: God, please help me today to work out any conflicts I still have with others.

DAY 2 PROVERBS 29:11

QUESTION: Are you controlled by your feelings?

___
___
___
___

PRAYER FOR THE DAY: God, please help me be like the wise man and not the fool.

**U9 L4
Family**

DAY 3 JAMES 1:19-20

QUESTION: Are you a good listener? (Ask your parents, other family members and friends.)

_____
_____
_____
_____

PRAYER FOR THE DAY: God, please help me listen to your word and to others. Help me understand how they feel.

DAY 4 2 CORINTHIANS 10:4-5

QUESTION: What attitude or mood do you have a hard time overcoming?

_____
_____
_____
_____

PRAYER FOR THE DAY: God, please help me to capture and hold on to every good thought and to capture and toss out all of the bad ones.

DAY 5 COLOSSIANS 3:13

QUESTION: Do you forgive quickly, or do you hold grudges?

_____
_____
_____
_____

PRAYER FOR THE DAY: God, please help me to forgive and forget quickly.

RESOLVING CONFLICT

WEEK 39

U9 L4
Family

DAY 6 EPHESIANS 4:15

QUESTION: When you tell someone the truth, do you say it because you love them or just because you want to make your point?

_____
_____
_____
_____

PRAYER FOR THE DAY: God, please help me speak with love and kindness today.

DAY 7 1 PETER 2:21-22

QUESTION: Look up the definition of "deceive." Do you mislead people into thinking that you're telling the truth, or do you tell the whole truth?

_____
_____
_____
_____

PRAYER FOR THE DAY: God, please help me be completely truthful when I speak.

WEEKLY CHALLENGE
(WRITE YOUR WEEKLY CHALLENGE AND HOW YOU FULFILLED IT.)

RESOLVING CONFLICT

U9 L4
Family

COMPASSION

MEMORY VERSE: Mark 1:41

Filled with compassion, Jesus reached out his hand and touched the man. "I am willing," he said. "Be clean!"

DAY 1 MARK 1:40-42

QUESTION: What is "compassion"?

_____
_____
_____
_____

PRAYER FOR THE DAY: God, please help me today to have compassion for other people like Jesus did.

DAY 2 MATTHEW 9:35-38

QUESTION: Why do you think Jesus had compassion on the crowds of people around him?

_____
_____
_____
_____

PRAYER FOR THE DAY: God, help me to have a heart filled with compassion today.

WEEK 40

**U10 L1
The Character
of Jesus II**

DAY 3 MATTHEW 14:13-14

QUESTION: Because Jesus was filled with compassion, what did he do for those who were sick?

_____
_____
_____
_____

PRAYER FOR THE DAY: God, please help me to do something today to help someone in need.

DAY 4 MARK 6:32-34

QUESTION: Because Jesus was filled with compassion, what did he do for these people?

_____
_____
_____
_____

PRAYER FOR THE DAY: God, please help me to talk about you to someone I see today.

DAY 5 PSALM 145:8-9

QUESTION: Who does God have compassion for?

_____
_____
_____
_____

PRAYER FOR THE DAY: God, thank you so much for being a loving Father who cares about what happens to me today.

COMPASSION

WEEK 40

**U10 L1
The Character
of Jesus II**

DAY 6 ISAIAH 30:18

QUESTION: Does God want to be compassionate to us? Why?

_____
_____
_____
_____

PRAYER FOR THE DAY: God, thank you so much for your compassion on me.

DAY 7 2 CORINTHIANS 1:3-4

QUESTION: Why should you pray when you are going through times of trouble?

_____
_____
_____
_____

PRAYER FOR THE DAY: God, please help me to comfort someone who is going through a hard time today.

WEEKLY CHALLENGE
(WRITE YOUR WEEKLY CHALLENGE AND HOW YOU FULFILLED IT.)

COMPASSION

WEEK 40

U10 L1
The Character of Jesus II

SELF-CONTROL

MEMORY VERSE: Galatians 5:22-23

But the fruit of the Spirit is love, joy, peace, patience, kindness, goodness, faithfulness, gentleness and self-control. Against such things there is no law.

DAY 1 GALATIANS 5:22-23

QUESTION: How have you learned that self-control is a part of the Holy Spirit?

___
___
___
___

PRAYER FOR THE DAY: Lord, help me to show self-control so that others can see your Spirit today.

DAY 2 PROVERBS 25:28

QUESTION: Stone walls were used to protect cities against enemies. How is it when you don't use self-control that you are like an unprotected city?

___
___
___
___

PRAYER FOR THE DAY: Lord, help me to use self-control today and see how you bless me.

WEEK 41

**U10 L2
The Character
of Jesus II**

DAY 3 PROVERBS 14:16-17

QUESTION: Have you been hot-headed or easily angered? How?

_____
_____
_____
_____

PRAYER FOR THE DAY: Lord, let me trust you instead of becoming angry.

DAY 4 PROVERBS 15:18

QUESTION: How can patience calm a quarrel (argument)?

_____
_____
_____
_____

PRAYER FOR THE DAY: Lord, remind me to be patient, so I can help to stop an argument today.

DAY 5 2 PETER 1:5-7

QUESTION: How are you adding self-control to your life?

_____
_____
_____
_____

PRAYER FOR THE DAY: Lord, let me please you by growing in self-control.

SELF-CONTROL

WEEK 41

**U10 L2
The Character
of Jesus II**

DAY 6 1 PETER 4:7

QUESTION: How does a lack of self-control keep you from praying?

_____
_____
_____
_____

PRAYER FOR THE DAY: Lord, thank you for allowing us to pray to you...and for listening and answering!

DAY 7 1 PETER 1:13

QUESTION: How will you prepare your mind for action today?

_____
_____
_____
_____

PRAYER FOR THE DAY: Lord, thank you for the fruit of self-control. Help me to be prepared for anything that comes my way today.

WEEKLY CHALLENGE

(WRITE YOUR WEEKLY CHALLENGE AND HOW YOU FULFILLED IT.)

SELF-CONTROL

**U10 L2
The Character
of Jesus II**

PATIENCE

MEMORY VERSE: Romans 12:12

Be joyful in hope, patient in affliction, faithful in prayer.

DAY 1 JOHN 18:25-27, ACTS 2:14-16

QUESTION: How was Peter changed because Jesus chose to forgive him?

_____
_____
_____
_____

PRAYER FOR THE DAY: Lord, help me see how I can change and serve others.

DAY 2 2 PETER 3:9

QUESTION: Why is God patient with you?

_____
_____
_____
_____

PRAYER FOR THE DAY: Lord, please help me to respond to your patience and build a strong relationship with you.

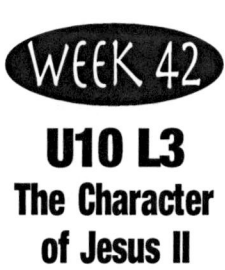

WEEK 42

**U10 L3
The Character
of Jesus II**

DAY 3 EPHESIANS 4:2

QUESTION: What does it mean for you to "bear with someone in love"?

_____
_____
_____
_____

PRAYER FOR THE DAY: Lord, show me today what I need to change in order to bear with others in love.

DAY 4 EPHESIANS 4:32

QUESTION: When do you find it hard to forgive?

_____
_____
_____
_____

PRAYER FOR THE DAY: Lord, strengthen my faith so that I will be ready to forgive.

DAY 5 MARK 11:25

QUESTION: In what ways has God forgiven you?

_____
_____
_____
_____

PRAYER FOR THE DAY: Lord, thank you for forgiving me. Help me to forgive others.

PATIENCE

WEEK 42

**U10 L3
The Character
of Jesus II**

DAY 6 LUKE 9:52-56

QUESTION: Who can you forgive even while they have something still to change or understand?

_____
_____
_____
_____

PRAYER FOR THE DAY: Lord, help me to forgive people when they do hurtful things to me today.

DAY 7 ROMANS 8:25

QUESTION: What is something God wants me to hope and wait patiently for?

_____
_____
_____
_____

PRAYER FOR THE DAY: Lord, thank you for your faithfulness that helps me wait.

WEEKLY CHALLENGE
(WRITE YOUR WEEKLY CHALLENGE AND HOW YOU FULFILLED IT.)

PATIENCE

**U10 L3
The Character
of Jesus II**

ANGER

MEMORY VERSE: James 1:19-20

My dear brothers, take note of this: Everyone should be quick to listen, slow to speak and slow to become angry, for man's anger does not bring about the righteous life that God desires.

DAY 1 JOHN 2:12-17

QUESTION: Why was Jesus angry when he saw men selling animals in the temple courts? Do you ever get angry because someone is doing something wrong?

___
___
___
___

PRAYER FOR THE DAY: God, please help me have zeal for you today.

DAY 2 PROVERBS 16:32

QUESTION: When Jesus got angry, he did not sin. This is hard for us. What usually makes you angry? Why should you control your temper?

___
___
___
___

PRAYER FOR THE DAY: God, help me to control my temper today.

U10 L4
The Character of Jesus II

DAY 3 PROVERBS 15:1

QUESTION: How can speaking in a kind and gentle way help someone else not get angry?

_____
_____
_____
_____

PRAYER FOR THE DAY: God, help me to speak with kind and gentle words today.

DAY 4 PROVERBS 29:11

QUESTION: Is it wise or foolish to keep yourself and your temper under control? Why?

_____
_____
_____
_____

PRAYER FOR THE DAY: God, help me to set a good example today in all I do.

DAY 5 JAMES 1:19

QUESTION: What does it mean to be "quick to listen and slow to become angry"?

_____
_____
_____
_____

PRAYER FOR THE DAY: God, help me to be a good listener all day.

ANGER

WEEK 43

**U10 L4
The Character
of Jesus II**

DAY 6 MATTHEW 12:33-35

QUESTION: The things we say come out of our hearts. Why is it important to have good things from God in our hearts?

_____
_____
_____
_____

PRAYER FOR THE DAY: God, help me have your words in my heart so good things will come out of my mouth.

DAY 7 COLOSSIANS 3:1-2

QUESTION: How can you set your heart and mind on God and Christ?

_____
_____
_____
_____

PRAYER OF THE DAY: God, help me to ask myself "What would Jesus do?" so I can keep my heart and mind on Christ today.

WEEKLY CHALLENGE
(WRITE YOUR WEEKLY CHALLENGE AND HOW YOU FULFILLED IT.)

ANGER

**U10 L4
The Character
of Jesus II**

THANKFULNESS

MEMORY VERSE: Colossians 1:3

We always thank God, the Father of our Lord Jesus Christ, when we pray for you.

DAY 1 MATTHEW 14:18-21

QUESTION: Why did Jesus give thanks for the fish and the loaves?

_____
_____
_____
_____

PRAYER FOR THE DAY: God, help me to be thankful today for everything I have.

DAY 2 MARK 8:6-9

QUESTION: How many times did Jesus give thanks to God in this passage?

_____
_____
_____
_____

PRAYER FOR THE DAY: God, help me to say, "Thank you," often to those around me today.

WEEK 44

**U10 L5
The Character
of Jesus II**

DAY 3 HEBREWS 13:15-16

QUESTION: When you are really thankful, how do you act?
___
___
___
___

PRAYER FOR THE DAY: God, help me to show by my actions today that I am a thankful person.

DAY 4 COLOSSIANS 1:3

QUESTION: Which people should you thank God for today?
___
___
___
___

PRAYER FOR THE DAY: God, help me to be a person who is thankful for the people you have put in my life.

DAY 5 COLOSSIANS 3:17

QUESTION: How can you show your family and the people at school that you love God and that you are a thankful person?
___
___
___
___

PRAYER FOR THE DAY: God, help my actions show that I love you and that I am thankful.

THANKFULNESS

WEEK 44

U10 L5
The Character of Jesus II

DAY 6 COLOSSIANS 4:2

QUESTION: What does it mean to be devoted to prayer?

_____
_____
_____
_____

PRAYER FOR THE DAY: God, help me to love to pray to you.

DAY 7 JOHN 11:38-44

QUESTION: Was Jesus thankful that God answered his prayers? Why?

_____
_____
_____
_____

PRAYER OF THE DAY: God, help me to be thankful for all the prayers you have answered in my life.

WEEKLY CHALLENGE
(WRITE YOUR WEEKLY CHALLENGE AND HOW YOU FULFILLED IT.)

THANKFULNESS

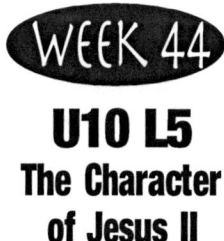

**U10 L5
The Character
of Jesus II**

MEDICAL SCIENCE AND THE BIBLE

MEMORY VERSE: Psalm 139:13-14

For you created my inmost being;
  you knit me together in my mother's womb.
I praise you because I am fearfully and wonderfully made;
  your works are wonderful, I know that full well.

DAY 1 LEVITICUS 11:4-8

QUESTION: Why do you think God wanted his people to stay away from eating these specific animals?

_____
_____
_____

PRAYER FOR THE DAY: God, thank you for creating laws that help me to stay healthy.

Did you know? Diseases like salmonella and botulism come from meats that are not cooked thoroughly.

DAY 2 LEVITICUS 11:13-19

QUESTION: Why do you think that God wanted his people to stay away from these birds and not eat them?

_____
_____
_____

PRAYER FOR THE DAY: God, help me to see all the benefits of your divine laws.

Did you know? The birds (and the bats) listed in the scripture could not be eaten because they often fed on dead animals and could give the people diseases.

WEEK 45

U11 L1
Evidences II

DAY 3 NUMBERS 19:11-12

QUESTION: How do you show God you appreciate his laws?

_____
_____
_____

PRAYER FOR THE DAY: God, help me to show how much I appreciate your laws by being eager to obey you today.

Did you know? Dr. Ignaz Semmelweis (who discovered that the high death rate in his hospital could be reduced simply by doctors washing their hands) was driven into seclusion by his colleagues for his "outrageous" beliefs.

DAY 4 LEVITICUS 13:40-46

QUESTION: Why do you think God wanted infectious people to be isolated outside of camp?

_____
_____
_____

PRAYER FOR THE DAY: God, help me to see how science and the Bible go hand in hand.

Did you know? Moses has been called by some "the first microbiologist"! No one knew about bacteria, virus or germs, but God told the Israelites to bury, clean and isolate—methods for avoiding diseases.

DAY 5 LEVITICUS 13:47-52

QUESTION: What can you do around the house that will show your obedience to God's law?

_____
_____
_____

PRAYER FOR THE DAY: God, thank you that everything you tell me is for my own good.

Did you know? The Egyptians in Moses' time put worm blood or donkey manure on the infected spot caused by a splinter.

MEDICAL SCIENCE AND THE BIBLE

U11 L1
Evidences II

DAY 6 LEVITICUS 17:11

QUESTION: What can you do today to show God how much you appreciate your body?

_____
_____
_____

PRAYER FOR THE DAY: God, thank you for the blood that runs through my body, carrying the things I need to stay alive.

Did you know? Blood carries oxygen to all the cells and tissues in your body. In fact, 1/3 of the total blood pumped out of your heart brings oxygen to the brain.

DAY 7 GENESIS 17:5-12

QUESTION: What role did circumcision play in the relationship between God and his people?

_____
_____
_____

PRAYER FOR THE DAY: God, thank you for inspiring prophets like Moses and faithful men like Abraham, who showed us your divine love and knowledge through your laws.

Did you know? Research has shown that the eighth day is actually the most favorable time to circumcise a male infant. All of the factors required for blood clotting and healing of the wound reach optimum conditions on the eighth day. (Ask your parents to explain the practice of circumcision.)

WEEKLY CHALLENGE
(WRITE YOUR WEEKLY CHALLENGE AND HOW YOU FULFILLED IT.)

MEDICAL SCIENCE AND THE BIBLE

**U11 L1
Evidences II**

PHYSICAL SCIENCE AND THE BIBLE

MEMORY VERSE: Jeremiah 10:12

But God made the earth by his power;
he founded the world by his wisdom
and stretched out the heavens by his
understanding.

DAY 1 PSALM 102:23-27

QUESTION: How does it make you feel knowing that God will always stay the same?

_____
_____
_____

PRAYER FOR THE DAY: God, thank you that I can always rely on you.

Did you know? Scientists have proven that the physical universe is growing old, wearing out and running down.

DAY 2 JOB 36:27-29

QUESTION: What would happen if God had not provided a water cycle on Earth?

_____
_____
_____

PRAYER FOR THE DAY: God, help me remember you every time I see water.

Did you know? The Earth's surface is 70% water! Only two percent of it is available for drinking.

WEEK 46

U11 L2
Evidences II

DAY 3 AMOS 9:5-6

QUESTION: How would God take the waters of the sea and pour them out over the land?

_____
_____
_____

PRAYER FOR THE DAY: God, thank you for providing everything I need for life.

Did you know? The rain comes down and flows into rivers which feed the oceans. Then the water is evaporated, and wind currents blow it back over the continents as rain.

DAY 4 JONAH 2:1-6

QUESTION: Jonah experienced God's power over water and nature. How would you have felt if you were Jonah?

_____
_____
_____

PRAYER FOR THE DAY: God, thank you for the beauty and vastness of the ocean; they remind me of your power.

Did you know? There is an underwater mountain range in the Atlantic Ocean that is 10,000 miles long!

DAY 5 JOB 38:22-23

QUESTION: Where on earth does God have his storehouses of snow and ice?

_____
_____
_____

PRAYER FOR THE DAY: God, thank you for all the variety in weather!

Did you know? If all the snow and ice on earth were to melt, the oceans would rise 450-800 feet!

PHYSICAL SCIENCE AND THE BIBLE

WEEK 46

**U11 L2
Evidences II**

DAY 6 ISAIAH 40:12-13

QUESTION: If God even gave dust a purpose, how much greater is God's purpose for you?

_____
_____
_____

PRAYER FOR THE DAY: God, help me to appreciate both your plans for me and your plans for the things on earth!

Did you know? Without dust, rain and snow could not form!

DAY 7 GENESIS 6:9-15

QUESTION: In what ways can you strive to be more righteous like Noah?

_____
_____
_____

PRAYER FOR THE DAY: God, thank you for giving me the same opportunity to be saved as Noah.

Did you know? The dimensions of Noah's ark have been found to be the most seaworthy ratio for a ship.

WEEKLY CHALLENGE
(WRITE YOUR WEEKLY CHALLENGE AND HOW YOU FULFILLED IT.)

PHYSICAL SCIENCE AND THE BIBLE

U11 L2
Evidences II

ARCHAEOLOGY AND THE O.T.

MEMORY VERSE: Joshua 4:21-22

He said to the Israelites, "In the future when your descendants ask their fathers, 'What do these stones mean?' tell them, 'Israel crossed the Jordan on dry ground.'"

DAY 1 GENESIS 11:4-6

QUESTION: What happens when people are unified?
___
___
___

PRAYER FOR THE DAY: God, please help me to be unified with my friends at church

Did you know? The word "Babel" comes from the words Bab-El. The meaning of this word is not "confusion" but "Gate of God."

DAY 2 GENESIS 12:1-4

QUESTION: How would you react if God asked you to leave your family and move to another country?
___
___
___

PRAYER FOR THE DAY: God, please teach me to be willing to obey your will for my life.

Did you know? In 1922, Ur was excavated. Before this, many people thought Ur never existed; therefore, they did not believe that Abraham existed.

WEEK 47

U11 L3
Evidences II

DAY 3 GENESIS 7:24-8:3

QUESTION: Noah was on the ark for over a year. How would you react to being on a boat for that long?

_____
_____
_____

PRAYER FOR THE DAY: God, please help me to fully trust you to take care of my life.

Did you know? Practically every ancient nation or tribe in the world has its own flood story, many of them amazingly similar to the biblical account.

DAY 4 GENESIS 50:1-3

QUESTION: How much do you think Joseph loved his father? What can you do to show love to your family?

_____
_____
_____

PRAYER FOR THE DAY: God, please help me to love my family.

Did you know? The reason they mourned for Jacob for seventy days was because it took that long for the embalming process to be completed.

DAY 5 EXODUS 19:5-6

QUESTION: How does it make you feel to know that you are God's treasured possession?

_____
_____
_____

PRAYER FOR THE DAY: God, please help me to always remember that I am treasured and loved by you.

Did you know? Critics thought the art of writing was unknown in Moses' day. But great libraries were found in Ur, showing that people could write in even Abraham's day.

ARCHAEOLOGY AND THE O.T.

U11 L3
Evidences II

DAY 6 JOSHUA 1:1-5

QUESTION: How would you feel if God had come to you and asked you to do this great task?

_____
_____
_____

PRAYER FOR THE DAY: God, thank you that you choose to work through me!

Did you know? There is more proof of the Hebrew conquest of Canaan than the Norman conquest of England (1066 A.D.).

DAY 7 2 CHRONICLES 9:22-24

QUESTION: What do you think made Solomon so great in wisdom?

_____
_____
_____

PRAYER FOR THE DAY: God, please help me to understand your word and to apply it to my life today.

Did you know: The stables that King Solomon built to house his chariot horses were found in Megiddo.

WEEKLY CHALLENGE
(WRITE YOUR WEEKLY CHALLENGE AND HOW YOU FULFILLED IT.)

ARCHAEOLOGY AND THE O.T.

WEEK 47

U11 L3
Evidences II

ARCHAEOLOGY AND THE N.T.

MEMORY VERSE: Romans 10:17

Consequently, faith comes from hearing the message, and the message is heard through the word of Christ.

DAY 1 MATTHEW 4:1-4

QUESTION: How did Jesus use God's word to fight Satan?
_____
_____
_____

PRAYER FOR THE DAY: God, help me to fight temptations in my life with your powerful word.

Did you know? At the highest point of Herod's Temple, where Satan took Jesus, there was a 100-foot drop to the Kidron Valley.

DAY 2 JOHN 9:1-7

QUESTION: In what ways can you see God's work displayed in your life?
_____
_____
_____

PRAYER FOR THE DAY: God, thank you for working in my life. Help me to be grateful for all your blessings.

Did you know? The pool of Siloam was used as part of a major water system. It was developed by King Hezekiah.

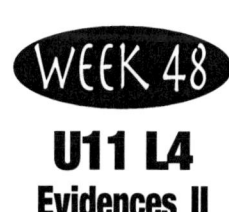

U11 L4
Evidences II

DAY 3 JOHN 5:6-9

QUESTION: In what ways do you procrastinate about doing God's will? Do you make excuses to avoid following instructions from your parents?

_____
_____

PRAYER FOR THE DAY: God, please help me to be obedient to your commands and to do the things my parents ask me to do—without making excuses.

Did you know? The pools of Bethesda are located near the present day Saint-Annes church in Jerusalem.

DAY 4 JOHN 4:13-1

QUESTION: Do you thirst more for God's word and his righteousness, or for material possessions?

_____
_____

PRAYER FOR THE DAY: God, help me to see that your word provides me with everything I need to be happy.

Did you know? Jacob's well was cleaned out in 1935—it was found to be 138 feet deep!

DAY 5 JOHN 18:2-5

QUESTION: Jesus had courage to face being arrested. Do you have the courage to tell others about Jesus, even if it could mean losing some friends?

_____
_____

PRAYER FOR THE DAY: God, please help me to have courage and not be ashamed of telling others about Jesus.

Did you know? The Gihon Spring, located in the Kidron Valley, was redirected by Hezekiah's tunnel into the Pool of Siloam. This tunnel was a major water system.

ARCHAEOLOGY AND THE N.T.

WEEK 48

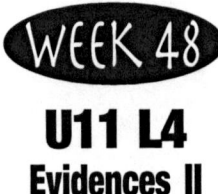

U11 L4
Evidences II

DAY 6 MATTHEW 26:36-41

QUESTION: For how long did Jesus pray? Why?
___
___
___

PRAYER FOR THE DAY: God, help me to be like Jesus, praying whenever I feel troubled, sad or upset.

Did you know? The name "Gethsemane" means "oil press." It was a place for squeezing the oil from olives.

DAY 7 1 CORINTHIANS 9:24-27

QUESTION: Are you making every effort to get close to God?
___
___
___

PRAYER FOR THE DAY: God, please help me to run toward you with all of my heart.

Did you know? The foot race that is talked about in this scripture is called the "Isthimian Games" which took place every other year. The prize was a leafy wreath.

WEEKLY CHALLENGE
(WRITE YOUR WEEKLY CHALLENGE AND HOW YOU FULFILLED IT.)

ARCHAEOLOGY AND THE N.T.

U11 L4
Evidences II

FULFILLED PROPHECIES

MEMORY VERSE: Luke 24:44

He said to them, "This is what I told you while I was still with you: Everything must be fulfilled that is written about me in the Law of Moses, the Prophets and the Psalms."

DAY 1 ISAIAH 53:3

QUESTION: Jesus let himself be hurt by other people. He knows what it is like to be sad. Can you think of a time when someone hurt you?

_____
_____
_____

PRAYER FOR THE DAY: Father, thank you for understanding how I feel, and for caring about it.

DAY 2 ISAIAH 53:6

QUESTION: We all sin and turn away from God. We often think our way is better than God's way. Think of something you can do *God's way* today.

_____
_____
_____

PRAYER FOR THE DAY: Dear God, thank you for sending Jesus to die on the cross. Help me today to live and act in a way that follows Jesus' example.

WEEK 49

**U12 L1
Crucifixion and Resurrection**

DAY 3 ISAIAH 53:7

QUESTION: Jesus did not fight back or argue when he was crucified. How can you imitate him today?

_____
_____
_____

PRAYER FOR THE DAY: Father, thank you for letting me know I can be like Jesus in every situation. Help me to trust you in the hardest times, just as he did.

DAY 4 ISAIAH 53:12

QUESTION: Even though Jesus died on the cross, God let him become great and strong. Think of something you can do to sacrifice today.

_____
_____
_____

PRAYER FOR THE DAY: Father, thank you for giving Jesus the victory, that he could rise from the dead. Thanks for teaching me that following you always ends in victory.

DAY 5 PSALM 22:1A

QUESTION: These are the words that Jesus cried out on the cross. What do you think it was like for Jesus to be abandoned by God?

_____
_____
_____

PRAYER FOR THE DAY: Dear God, thank you that Jesus was willing to be abandoned by you so that I will never have to be.

FULFILLED PROPHECIES

**U12 L1
Crucifixion and Resurrection**

DAY 6 PSALM 22:7-8

QUESTION: When Jesus hung on the cross people made fun of him, which probably hurt his feelings. What are the things you do that hurt Jesus?

_____
_____
_____

PRAYER FOR THE DAY: Dear God, please help me do things today that are loving. Please help me to please you, not hurt you.

DAY 7 JOHN 12:24-25

QUESTION: Jesus calls us to give our lives up the way he did. How can you give your life to God today?

_____
_____
_____

PRAYER FOR DAY: Dear God, thank you for giving Jesus to love us and be the best example for us. Help me follow you today the way Jesus did.

WEEKLY CHALLENGE
(WRITE YOUR WEEKLY CHALLENGE AND HOW YOU FULFILLED IT.)

FULFILLED PROPHECIES

WEEK 49

**U12 L1
Crucifixion and Resurrection**

THE GARDEN AND THE TRIAL

MEMORY VERSE: Matthew 26:39

Going a little farther, he fell with his face to the ground and prayed, "My Father, if it is possible, may this cup be taken from me. Yet not as I will, but as you will."

DAY 1 MATTHEW 26:36-39

QUESTION: Jesus feels overwhelmed with sorrow. Instead of giving in to this emotion and feeling sorry for himself, what does he do? How can you imitate Jesus?

_____
_____
_____

PRAYER FOR THE DAY: Father, thank you that Jesus can relate to me when I feel overwhelmed. Help me to remember to imitate him by praying through these times.

DAY 2 MATTHEW 26:39-42

QUESTION: Jesus did what was right in spite of his feelings. What are some situations in which you need to do what is right no matter how you feel?

_____
_____
_____

PRAYER FOR THE DAY: Father, thank you that you will give me the courage to do what is right.

WEEK 50

**U12 L2
Crucifixion and Resurrection**

DAY 3 MATTHEW 26:47-50

QUESTION: Judas betrayed Jesus with a kiss, which is generally thought of as a sign of friendship. How can we make sure that our loyalty to Jesus will be true?

_____
_____
_____

PRAYER FOR THE DAY: Father, thank you that I can be free from deceitfulness. Please help me to be open with others about my life and try to always be genuine in my relationship with you.

DAY 4 JOHN 17:1-8

QUESTION: What are the things Jesus accomplished?

_____
_____
_____

PRAYER FOR THE DAY: Father, thank you that Jesus always finished what he started. Help me to be a great "finisher."

DAY 5 JOHN 17:9-26

QUESTION: Concerning his disciples, what did Jesus pray?

_____
_____
_____

PRAYER FOR THE DAY: Father, thank you for your power. I pray to use this power to be unified with other disciples and to grow in understanding spiritual things.

THE GARDEN AND THE TRIAL

WEEK 50

**U12 L2
Crucifixion and Resurrection**

DAY 6 MATT 26:59-66

QUESTION: Some people said false things about Jesus. Some people will say false things about you because of your faith. How should you react?

_____
_____
_____

PRAYER FOR THE DAY: Father, please help me to care more about what you think than about what others think.

DAY 7 JOHN 18:33-40

QUESTION: When Jesus says in verse 37, "everyone on the side of truth listens to me," what did he mean? In what ways can you be on the side of truth?

_____
_____
_____

PRAYER FOR THE DAY: Father, thank you for giving us the truth in your word. Please help me to love the truth and live it in my words and my actions

WEEKLY CHALLENGE
(WRITE YOUR WEEKLY CHALLENGE AND HOW YOU FULFILLED IT.)

THE GARDEN AND THE TRIAL

WEEK 50

U12 L2
Crucifixion and Resurrection

THE CROSS

MEMORY VERSE: Romans 5:6

You see, at just the right time, when we were still powerless, Christ died for the ungodly.

DAY 1 1 PETER 2:23

QUESTION: Jesus did not try to fight back when he was crucified. How can you have the same attitude and not fight back?

_____
_____
_____

PRAYER FOR THE DAY: God, please help me to not fight back when people are against me. Help me to be self-controlled on the inside and on the outside.

DAY 2 2 CORINTHIANS 5:15

QUESTION: Jesus died so that we will live for God and not for ourselves. Think of one way you can live for God today.

_____
_____
_____

PRAYER FOR THE DAY: Father, help me think of the best way to live for you today. Help me to remember this all day long.

WEEK 51

**U12 L3
Crucifixion and Resurrection**

DAY 3 GALATIANS 2:20

QUESTION: Jesus gave himself for us because he loved us. What's one way you can let Christ live in you today?

_____
_____
_____

PRAYER FOR THE DAY: Father, I want Jesus to live in me in some way today. Help me to see how to do this.

DAY 4 1 CORINTHIANS 1:18

QUESTION: Knowing about the cross is knowing about the power of God. Think of some area in which you want to be stronger and how the message of the cross can help.

_____
_____
_____

PRAYER FOR THE DAY: Father, since you had the power to raise Jesus from the dead, I know you have the power to help me change anything in my life. Please help me to _____.

DAY 5 1 JOHN 3:16

QUESTION: God showed us what love is by letting Jesus die for us. How can you love someone today by "laying down" your life for them?

_____
_____
_____

PRAYER FOR THE DAY: Father, thanks for teaching me to treat others as more important than myself.

THE CROSS

WEEK 51

**U12 L3
Crucifixion and
Resurrection**

DAY 6 HEBREWS 12:2

QUESTION: Even though dying on the cross hurt, Jesus knew that there would be joy later. What kind of "joy" can you expect if you decide to live like Jesus did?

_____
_____
_____

PRAYER FOR THE DAY: Father, thanks for letting me know that living like Jesus will help me to live a life that is full of joy.

DAY 7 PHILIPPIANS 2:5-11

QUESTION: Jesus was always obedient, even when it meant he had to die on the cross. How can you change to be more obedient at home?

_____
_____
_____

PRAYER FOR THE DAY: God, it's hard for me to always be obedient. Thanks for giving me Jesus as an example I can think of when I am having a hard time.

WEEKLY CHALLENGE
(WRITE YOUR WEEKLY CHALLENGE AND HOW YOU FULFILLED IT.)

THE CROSS

WEEK 51

**U12 L3
Crucifixion and
Resurrection**

THE RESURRECTION

MEMORY VERSE: Acts 2:36

"Therefore let all Israel be assured of this: God has made this Jesus, whom you crucified, both Lord and Christ."

DAY 1 MATTHEW 28:1-3

QUESTION: Everything about the resurrection showed the power of God. In what areas of your life do you want to use God's power?

_____
_____
_____

PRAYER FOR THE DAY: Father, thank you for being so powerful. Please help me to trust you when things seem hard and to remember that you can do anything.

DAY 2 MATTHEW 28:4

QUESTION: Why do you think that people were often afraid when they saw angels?

_____
_____
_____

PRAYER FOR THE DAY: Father, the angels showed these men how powerful you are. Help me not to be afraid of you, but to love you.

WEEK 52

**U12 L4
Crucifixion and Resurrection**

DAY 3 MATTHEW 28:5-8

QUESTION: Who can you share with today about how your life is different because of Jesus?

_____
_____
_____

PRAYER FOR THE DAY: Father, thank you for Jesus and the fact that he was willing to die so that I could have a chance to live. Please help me to share my life today with a friend who doesn't know you.

DAY 4 MATTHEW 28:9-10

QUESTION: Jesus said to not be afraid. How do you feel when you are afraid to do something? Do you pray to God for help?

_____
_____
_____

PRAYER FOR THE DAY: Father, thank you for how powerful you are. Please help me to pray to you when I am afraid.

DAY 5 MATTHEW 28:11-15

QUESTION: Many lies and theories about the resurrection have been around for years, but the truth is that Jesus *did* rise from the dead. How does that make you feel?

_____
_____
_____

PRAYER FOR THE DAY: Father, thank you that I can know for sure that I can know that the Bible is always correct!

THE RESURRECTION

WEEK 52

**U12L4
Crucifixion and
Resurrection**

DAY 6 MATTHEW 28:16-17

QUESTION: When all the disciples saw Jesus, they worshiped (loved and honored) him; but even then, some doubted. What are some ways that you have clearly seen God but then doubted?

_____
_____
_____

PRAYER FOR THE DAY: Father, thank you that you hear me and work to show yourself in my life. Please help me not to doubt you and your word.

DAY 7 MATTHEW 28:18-20

QUESTION: What are some ways you can help people to become disciples? Pray about it, and go for it!

_____
_____
_____

PRAYER FOR THE DAY: Father, thank you for caring for me and allowing me to know your word. Help me to listen to you and to obey right away.

WEEKLY CHALLENGE
(WRITE YOUR WEEKLY CHALLENGE AND HOW YOU FULFILLED IT.)

THE RESURRECTION

**U12L4
Crucifixion and Resurrection**

LOOKING BACK, LOOKING AHEAD

There is a time for looking back and a time for looking ahead.

Take a few minutes first to look back ➜
Turn to the beginning of this book, to Day 1, and thumb through it, glancing at some of the responses you have written during the past year. Then think about how much you have learned about God, about how much he loves you, about living for him, about sharing him with others. Realize that you have memorized many verses that will help you in years to come.

Why are you glad you spent time with God during this past year?

Now, let's look ahead ➜
Next year you will also have a quiet time book to help you study the Bible and grow in your prayer life. What did you learn from last year that you want to put into practice as you begin a new year spending time with God daily?

_____
_____
_____
_____

What commitment will you make to God for this new year?

_____
_____
_____
_____

Remember, God loves you and is your greatest fan!

CPSIA information can be obtained at www.ICGtesting.com
260507BV00001B/2/A